JACK KEROUAC

and the

Whiz Kids

DIVERSE ESSAYS FOR
DIVERSE READERS

ROGER ZOTTI

Jack Kerouac and the Whiz Kids: Diverse Essays for Diverse Readers
Copyright © 2021 Roger Zotti.

Produced and printed
by Stillwater River Publications.
All rights reserved. Written and produced in the
United States of America.
This book may not be reproduced
or sold in any form without the expressed, written
permission of the author and publisher.

Visit our website at
www.StillwaterPress.com
for more information.

First Stillwater River Publications Edition
Library of Congress Control Number: 2020922434
Paperback ISBN: 978-1-952521-87-4
Hardcover ISBN: 978-1-952521-89-8
1 2 3 4 5 6 7 8 9 10
Written by Roger Zotti
Published by Stillwater River Publications,
Pawtucket, RI, USA.

Publisher's Cataloging-In-Publication Data
(Prepared by The Donohue Group, Inc.)

Names: Zotti, Roger, author.

Title: Jack Kerouac and the Whiz Kids : diverse essays
for diverse readers / Roger Zotti.

Description: First Stillwater River Publications edi-
tion. | Pawtucket, RI, USA : Stillwater River
Publications, [2021]

Identifiers: ISBN 9781952521874 (paperback) |
ISBN 9781952521898 (hardcover)

Subjects: LCSH: Kerouac, Jack, 1922-1969. | Popular
culture. | Chicago White Sox (Baseball team) |
Books--Reviews. | LCGFT: Essays.

Classification: LCC PS3626.O88 J33 2021 | DDC
814/.6--dc23

To Maryann, Tom, Leslie, Katja, Roy, and Jake.

... words are just so important to me.
Words can become emotional tattoos.
If somebody says something beautiful to you,
you can remember it forever.

~Janet McTeer

Ultimately, literature is nothing but carpentry.
With both you are working with reality,
a material just as hard as wood.

~Gabriel Garcia Marquez

The failure to read good books both enfeebles the vision and
strengthens our most fatal tendency —
the belief that the here and now is all there is.

~Allan Bloom

A classic is something that everybody wants to have read
and nobody wants to read.

~Mark Twain

Table of Contents

INTRODUCTION

I n his book *Writing about Your Life: A Journey into the Past,* the late William Zinsser says: "All writing is talking to someone else on paper. Talk like yourself." To talk like myself was my first goal in writing *Jack Kerouac and the Whiz Kids.*

My second goal was to entertain readers because, as T.S. Eliot said, "Entertainment enlarges the sympathies, stimulates the mind and the spirit, warms the heart, punctures the balloons of hypocrisy, greed, and sham, tickles the funny bone, and leaves us with the glow that comes when we have been well entertained."

That readers will be gently informed by the diverse essays in this book was my third goal.

SOME FROST

Compared with the more intense British procedurals, like *George Gently, Silent Witness,* and *Line of Duty, A Touch of Frost,* which aired from 1992 to 2010, treated viewers to moments of comic relief in each episode.

Take season nine's "Mistaken Identity" episode. In it, Frost (David Jason) meets Ronnie Lonnegan (Michelle Joseph), his new assistant. He assumes Ronnie is Irish. No, Ronnie isn't Irish. He assumes Ronnie is a man. No, Ronnie isn't a man but an intelligent, attractive woman of color.

Of course Frost is surprised the first time he sees her. "What the hell are you doing in my office?" he blurts out. The reliable DS George Toolan (John Lyons) is with Frost and softly tells him that she's Ronnie Lonnegan.

Frost: Sorry. Sorry about that. My mistake.

Ronnie: Ronnie Lonnegan.

Frost: Ah! Ronnie. Ronnie Lonnegan. Reminds me... It sounds like Lonnie Donegan... You remember Lonnie Donegan, don't you, George? You remember him? That skiffle player...You know that song he had: (Singing) "Does your chewing gum lose its flavor on the bedpost over—?" (Pause) Are you, ah, normally in mufti? Are you, Ronnie?

Ronnie: Temporary attachment here, guv. I've been working undercover for several months in London.

Frost: Nice to have a splash of color around here. (Pause). Sorry, all I meant was—

Ronnie: (Smiling) I know what you mean, guv.

Nor does a day go by without some kind of conflict, often dryly humorous, between Frost and his superior, Superintendent Norman Mullet (Bruce Alexander). The reason? They're total opposites. Mullet's primary concern is the staff's image, which must be pristine in the public's eyes. Protocol must be followed.

On the other hand, to Mullet's chagrin, Frost doesn't give a hoot about image and protocol.

There are times, however, when Mullet isn't annoyed with Frost, especially when matters become serious.

Near the end of season fourteen's "Mind Games," Frost, seated at his desk, is seriously distressed because he's the reason why a man named Carl Meyer (the superb

Jonathan Slinger) has spent several years in prison for two murders he didn't commit.

Aware of Frost's anguish, Mullet enters the DI's office on the evening the real murderer has been caught. He tells Frost, "You can't blame yourself for what Chief Inspector Talbot [the previous inspector] didn't do."

Frost's response: "I should've listened to Carl. There was just so much evidence. I should have had doubts. That's my job."

In the scene we see how first-rate an actor Alexander is: He transforms Mullet's character into a compassionate individual, one we've rarely encountered and who clearly admires Frost for his dedication to his job, for his lack of pretense, for his honesty, and for his willingness to admit his mistakes.

Mullet confesses to Frost, "When I was a constable I was called to a domestic. A husband and wife row. I asked the wife if she wanted to leave. But they'd made up. He said he was sorry. She seemed all right. I don't know if I saw fear in her eyes as I left or if I imagined it afterwards. She was dead the next day. The husband set the house on fire. I can still see her face. (Pause) If you ever forget your mistakes, I think you're in the wrong job."

There's another pause, then Mullet says, "I'll be here if you want a lift."

JACK'S GLEE

J ack Kerouac's *Vanity of Duluoz: An Adventurous Education* (1935-1946) is written as if its main character and narrator Jack Duluoz, a thinly disguised Kerouac, is speaking to his wife. "All right, wifey," he begins, and continues addressing her for 280 pages.

Published in 1967, the settings of Kerouac's semi-autobiographical novel are his prep school days in Lowell, Massachusetts, his college life at Columbia University in New York City, his stint in the Navy during World War II, and the time he spent in jail in the early forties.

Did Someone Say Damon Runyon?

Kerouac's sense of glee is overlooked by critics and readers, or, as poet Allen Ginsburg puts it in *The Best Minds of My Generation*, his "enthusiasm or overflowing of feelings..." He praises Kerouac's novel as containing "some of his finest prose and most curious hindsights... This is one of his major novels and a departure from the romantic tradition."

A key scene exemplifying Kerouac's glee takes place in Dulouz's cell. Note, however, that Dulouz isn't really under arrest but, as a guard tells him, "all material witnesses to homicides are kept [in a cell]... you're simply what we call detained."

After a few days in his cell, Duluoz is visited by two inmates straight out of a Damon Runyon short story. Their names are Vincent "Falcon" Malatesta, who wears a black eye patch, and Joey Angeli, and they're professional hit men.

In the early forties Falcon was hired to kill Joey somewhere in New Jersey. The whack didn't take and somehow Angeli survived.

Six months later Joey had his revenge. In Chinatown, "Near the Scungili Restaurant, lo and behold," Falcon says, "I look up and there's Joe the Angel in the doorway. Boom, he shoots me in the eye." Falcon's friends cart him to the nearest hospital and it "turns out," he says, "the bullet went in and came out the other way without damaging the inner vittles of my brain."

Falcon explains to Duluoz, "We were paid to do these things, we got nothing personal against each other. We're just professionals. So here we are now standing up to one ninety-nine and two ninety-nine and a million years and we're the best of friends you ever saw. We're like soldiers, you get it."

With a shrug of his shoulders Duluoz replies, "That's great."

A Hijacker Named Yogi

Falcon and Joey leave Duluoz's cell and soon the muscular Yogi the Hijacker, another Runyon-like character, marches in.

> Yogi: Everybody here's mixed up with Murder Incorporated. They're all a bunch of bums. Kid, don't trust any of them. You can trust me, that's one sure thing. All I want to know from you is this: What that kid Claude the Maybreeze was; was he a schnook went for men's pants?

> Duluoz: No, not in the least. What the hell you expect him to find there?

> Yogi: Find something might interest him.

Trust Only Falcon

In the evening Falcon returns and wants to know if Claude is "a dilly dilly daisy? You know what I mean, a guy who waits around subway toilets for characters to come in?"

Duluoz emphatically says Claude is "just a regular kid who's good looking and got set upon by a homo."

Then Falcon tells Duluoz he shouldn't "trust anybody else in this joint, I'm Vincent Malatesta and I may be an assassin on pay but I'm honest, my father was an honest cabinetmaker. If you have any problems," Falcon continues, "come to me and tell me anything's on your mind anytime. And don't be afraid of me because of my black patch and my reputation."

Jack's Male Person

Later Joey Angeli appears and tells Duluoz not to trust Malatesta, "who's a nice guy" but "the only guy in here you can trust is me, Joey Angeli."

Then the conversation turns to Claude.

Joey: Did he ever feel up your leg with his knee?

Duluoz: No, and if he did try to feel up my leg with his knee, I wouldn't talk to him anymore.

Joey: That's funny, now why not?

Duluoz: Because I think it would add up to an insult to my person as a male person.

Joey: Well, that's well put.

Duluoz: [Claude] was a nineteen-year-old boy, who had been subject to an attempt at degrading by an older man who was a pederast, and he had

7

dispatched him off to an older lover called the river.

Two Joes

Kerouac is one of America's greatest visionary writers. For Ginsberg, the following passages from *Vanity of Duluoz* illustrate Kerouac's visionary writing and, at the same time, show him as his gleeful best:

First: "... I daydreamed that I was now going to go back to Columbia for my sophomore year, with home in New Haven, maybe near the Yale campus.... I was going to be such a sensational runner that we'd win every game against Dartmouth, Yale, Princeton, Harvard... and wind up in the Rose Bowl [where] I was going to run wild. Uncle Lou Lu Lubble for the first time in his life would throw his arms around me and weep.... The boys on the team would raise me up and in Rose Bowl's Pasadena Stadium and march me to the showers singing..."

Second: "I would idly turn my attention to winter indoor track and decide on the mile and run it under 4 flat (that was fast in those days.) So fast, indeed, that I'd be in the big meets at Madison Square Garden and beat the current great milers in final fantastic sprints bringing my time down to 3:50 flat. By this time everybody in the world is crying Duluoz! Duluoz!"

Third: "But, unsatisfied, I idly go out in the spring for the Columbia baseball team and bat homeruns clear over the Harlem River, one or two a game, including fast breaks from the bag to steal from first to second, from second to third, and finally, in the climactic game, from third to home, zip, slide, dust boom. Now the New York Yankees are after me. They want me to be their next Joe DiMaggio. I idly turn that down because I want Columbia to go to the Rose Bowl again in 1943. (Hah!)"

In the fourth passage, honestly, I nearly fell over laughing when I read it. Several "cigar-chewing guys" approached Duluoz and wanted to know if he'd start training to fight the great world heavyweight champion Joe Louis.

"I train idly in the Catskills," Duluoz tells us, "come down on a June night, face big tall Joe as the referee gives instructions, and then when the bell rings I rush out real fast and just pepper him real fast and so hard that he actually goes back bouncing over the ropes and into the third row and lays there knocked out."

As far as Duluoz is concerned, "I'm the world's heavyweight boxing champion, the greatest writer, the world's champ miler, Rose Bowl and (pro-bound with New York Giants football non pareil) now offered every job on every paper in New York, and what else? Tennis anyone?"

NEVER A BACKWARD STEP

Complicated guy that Ray "Boom Boom" Mancini, both in the boxing ring and out of it.

The former World Boxing Association lightweight champion in the 1980s began his professional boxing career in 1979 and retired in 1992 after a seventh round TKO loss to Greg Haugen. He compiled a 29-5-0 (23 KOs/KO by 3) record and was a television darling during his heyday in the 1980s.

Take a backward step? Not "Boom Boom."

For Mark Kriegel, in his scrupulously researched, brutally honest biography of Mancini, *The Good Son: The Life of Ray "Boom Boom" Mancini* (2010), Ray's life began spiraling downward after he defended his lightweight title on November 13, 1982, at Caesars Palace in Las Vegas, against a little-known twenty-three-year-old Korean named Duk Koo Kim.

Weeks before the fight Kim had predicted that "Either [Mancini] dies or I die." His words were prophetic. In the fourteenth round he was knocked out and died within days. Three months later his mother committed suicide.

In June 2010 Kim's son Chi-Wan, a dental student, and his fiancée Lee Young-Mee traveled to America to meet Mancini for the first time. They dined together, along with Ray's three children and his friend, actor Ed O'Neill, at Ray's Los Angeles home.

> Ray: I felt guilty because of your mother. I felt guilty that you never met your father. I didn't know they carried him out on a stretcher. It was a great fight. But after that there was nothing good about it... I had no love for it anymore. I was always looking for a way out.

> Chi-wan: It was better. For your health... Now I can tell you that when I saw the fight the first time I felt some hatred to you... But that, too, has passed... I think it was not your fault... Maybe now your family will be more happy.

> Ray: Thank you. Thank you for coming to America.

Prior to his meeting with Kim's son, Ray's life was in turmoil. Kriegel writes:

> "His eldest son wasn't speaking to him.

> "His daughter was locked up in Utah.

> "His wife had a boyfriend.

"He'd lost everything but the house. There he would rise and rule alone, all the while asking himself, 'What the fuck happened to my life?'"

But by the time Ray met Chi-wan and his fiancée, his life had changed for the better. "[Ray's daughter] Nina is considering a career in restaurant management," Kriegel writes. "The coming year will see [his son] Leonardo enroll at Santa Barbara Community College, and Ray-Ray [his youngest son] make varsity basketball as a high school sophomore."

Mancini vs. Bramble

Consider Mancini's two fights against Livingstone Bramble. In 1984, at Buffalo's Memorial Auditorium, Bramble, a 4-1 underdog, won the World Boxing Association lightweight title by stopping Mancini in the fourteenth round.

Born in Saint Croix, the British Virgin Islands, in 1960, Bramble cast himself as the villain against Mancini. His behavior was designed, Kriegel writes, "to unnerve Ray" and "to keep [him] seething with anger."

Kriegel quotes him as saying, "I made him think I had the voodoo. I tried to put everything in his mind: pit bulls and snakes. I wanted him to think I was crazy. I wanted him to hate my black ass."

Bramble even said Mancini was guilty of murdering Kim. "It doesn't matter if it happened in the ring. It's still murder."

Kriegel explains that "[Bramble's] purpose — 'to be the biggest jerk I could be' — was purely tactical. In fact, he regretted his behavior at the press conference. 'It wasn't nice,' he says. 'His parents were there, and they were devastated. But I had to do my job.'"

And he did.

And it worked.

As for the fight itself, Mancini was slightly ahead going into the fourteenth round, but he was noticeably fading and bleeding profusely from his right eye lid and nose. "Fifty-three seconds into the round," Kriegel writes, "with Ray on the ropes, his arms limp at his side," referee Marty Denkin stopped the fight. Mancini didn't protest, saying the referee was a "good guy. He gave me every chance."

Their second fight, at Reno, Nevada's Lawlor Events Center in 1985, went the fifteen-round distance, with Bramble winning a unanimous but close decision.

When it was over Bramble told Ray he respected him, that "I couldn't take the punishment I gave him. I would never try to measure my heart with his, never."

Also, he apologized to Ray's parents for disrespecting them.

When Mancini returned to the ring after a three-year absence, his opponent was tough Greg Haugen of Auburn, Washington. At stake was the North American Boxing Federation lightweight title.

"The whole press conference was about Ray," playwright Sam Kass is quoted as saying. "He was back in his glory. The words were flying. Then I look over at Haugen who's sitting off to the side with his wife.... No one wanted to talk to them. And Haugen was seething. *Seething*." He brought that controlled rage into the ring with him against Mancini.

It was evident from the opening round Mancini's timing was off. Way off. And his punches lacked power because he was pushing them.

Haugen fired a right-hand punch to Mancini's face in the seventh round that nearly took his head off. Though "Ray's lapse into unconsciousness was momentary," Kriegel writes, "he found himself trapped in the ropes, struggling like a bug in a web. He got to his feet, yes," but referee Mills Lane looked into his eyes and stopped the fight with thirty seconds remaining in the round. Mancini didn't protest. He knew his boxing career was over.

BESTS AND MORE BESTS

I've read many books about movies and actors, and Dale Thomajan's *From Cyd Charisse to Pyscho: A Book of Movie Bests* (1992) is one of the finest. Sure, it's opinionated — but that's precisely the author's purpose. As he writes in his introduction, "[This] is a book of opinions, my opinions — and it's quite possible *my* best will not always correspond to *your* best or *the* best. In other words, this book was written not to settle arguments but to start them."

Some of Thomajan's bests are "The Best Movie over Three Hours Long," "The Best Stylized Dialogue," "The Best MGM Musical Not to Involve Fred Astaire, Judy Garland, Gene Kelly, or Vincente Minnelli," "The Best Mad Scene," and "The Best Western Actor."

My three favorite Thomajan bests are "The Best Blonde," "The Best Actor," and "The Best Looking Human Being Ever to Appear on a Movie Screen."

Best Blonde? Marilyn Monroe? Maybe Jayne Mansfield or Shelley Winters? Answer: None of the aforementioned.

The winner is Joan Blondell. Yes, Thomajan writes, Joan Blondell, whose "specialties were, in her own words, 'the happy-go-lucky chorus girl, the saucy secretary, flip reporter, dumb-blonde waitress, I'll stick it to you broad.'"

The reason he picked Blondell, Thomajan says, occurred after he saw her in a 1930's flick where, in one scene, she "wrapped her arms around some Warner's contract player and kissed him. For the first and last time while watching a movie, I felt as if I were being kissed. (I can imagine how the actor felt.) Such were the empathetic powers of Joan Blondell."

Moving to Thomajan's choice of Best Actor, is it Olivier? Maybe Brando, Cagney, Grant, or Tracy? Sorry, none of the above. James Stewart is Thomajan's pick. Why? Few actors, Thomajan believes, could react the way Stewart did to a horrific incident in *The Man from Laramie*, director Anthony Mann's 1955 western.

Stewart's character, Will Lockhart, who, "after being restrained by bad-egg Alex Nicol's men, is shot through the hand by Nicol at point-blank range." What follows is the way Stewart "fixes his steel-blue eyes on Nicol and says, with as much pain and anger as any actor can be expected to summon, "Why you scum."

Another film exemplifying Stewart's acting skill is, Thomajan says, his work in Alfred Hitchcock's 1958 mystery-thriller *Vertigo*. He plays an ex-San Francisco police detective named Scottie Ferguson, who agrees to keep an eye on Madeleine Elster, an old college chum's wife. Her husband Gavin (the suave and sinister Tom Helmore) believes she's possessed by a dead woman's spirit.

"She'll be talking to me about something," Elster says to Ferguson. "Suddenly the words fade into silence. She's someone else. Someone I don't know."

Reluctantly, Ferguson accepts the assignment.

Elster, who co-owns a prosperous ship building business with his wife, knows that recently Ferguson and a cop were chasing a criminal over rooftops. While trying to save Ferguson, who had slipped, the cop fell to his death. Elster knows Ferguson blames himself for the police officer's death and is tortured by feelings of guilt.

The first time Ferguson sees Madeleine, or the woman he thinks is Madeleine, he becomes obsessed with her.

Of Stewart's performance Thomajan quotes film historian David Thomson: "Despite every hint of the darker side of Stewart, *Vertigo* was still a surprise and Stewart's performance is frightening in its intensity: a far cry from the man who talked to rabbits."

Now to Thomajan's choice of "The Best Looking Human Being Ever to Appear on a Movie Screen." She's a woman who has danced with Gene Kelly and Fred Astaire, who once called her "beautiful dynamite." She's Cyd Charisse.

In her tribute to Charisse, Verlyn Klinkenborg compares the dancer, who died in 2008 at age 86, with Judy Garland. "Again and again," she writes, "Garland lets the audience see, with a look, that she knows exactly what is going on, that life is really just a soundstage. But Charisse, who is the lesser actor by far, vanishes into the illusion, which is one of the things that made her such a perfect fit for Astaire."

Thomajan rightly believes Charisse possessed "erotic chic, and this, combined with her obvious taste and talent, is what made her not merely a great performer but an icon."

OL' BLUE EYES ROARS BACK

In early 1950, Frank Sinatra's career as a singer and musical comedy star was at an all-time low. His wife Barbara divorced him and MGM Studios dropped him. "The final straw came in April 1950," writes Tim Baker in a magazine piece titled "Second Chances," and occurred "on stage at New York's Copacabana nightclub, [when] a vocal-cord hemorrhage left the Chairman of the Board unable to produce any sound at all."

Sinatra was down.

But he wasn't out.

In 1952, Ava Gardner—she and Sinatra were married at the time—used her considerable star power to persuade dictatorial Columbia Pictures President Harry Cohn to test Sinatra for the role of Angelo Maggio in the screen version of *From Here to Eternity*, James Jones's best-selling novel.

Sinatra had read the book several times and believed he was born to play Maggio. The film's director, Fred Zinnemann, and its producer, Buddy Adler, didn't want him in the film. Their first choice was Eli Wallach, but he was committed to another project.

Sinatra did a screen test and it was extraordinary. "Frank improvised the saloon scene in which Maggio shakes dice and then casts them across a pool table. [He] used olives instead of dice," J. Randy Taraborrelli writes in *Sinatra: Behind the Legend*. "But that one gimmick wasn't all there was to Frank's performance. In fact, according to all accounts it was a commanding audition in every sense, part realistic, part theatrical."

Opening on August 5, 1953, at the Capitol Theatre in New York, Sinatra and the film — which also starred Burt Lancaster, Montgomery Clift, Deborah Kerr, and Donna Reed — won commercial and critical acclaim.

Fast forward to March 25, 1954, and the Pantages Theater in Los Angeles. Nominated for 1953's Best Supporting Actor, Sinatra faced some heady competition from Brandon deWilde (*Shane*), Eddie Albert (*Roman Holiday*), Jack Palance (*Shane*), and Robert Strauss (*Stalag 17*).

When Sinatra was announced as the winner, Taraborelli writes, "it was astonishing, in retrospect, that Frank Sinatra, basically known as a vocalist, would make one of the most dramatic comebacks in entertainment history as an actor."

Also, *From Here to Eternity* won the year's Oscar for Best Motion Picture.

One of the best books I've ever read about Sinatra is poet David Lehman's *Sinatra's Century: One Hundred Notes on the Man and His World*. Three key points he makes are, first, Sinatra couldn't read music. Not a note. "I learn songs by having them played for me a couple of times while I read the lyrics," he said. As for the lyrics, "I learn the lyrics by writing them out in long hand."

Second: Sinatra's singing voice is praised for its enunciation, but his speaking voice, Lehman says, has always been pure Hoboken.

Third: How did Sinatra liberate himself from his contract with Tommy Dorsey? According to Lehman, Dorsey's contract "would have obliged Sinatra to pay [him] one-third of all future earnings beyond a hundred bucks a week for the next ten years. An additional ten percent was earmarked for the bandleader's manager. "

Does the name Willie Moretti sound familiar? I hope it doesn't because Mr. Moretti and two of his, er, associates, paid Dorsey a visit one afternoon. They chatted for a time and, Dorsey said, "Willie fingered a gun and told me he was glad to hear that I was going to let Frank out of our deal. I took the hint."

Lehman points out "going solo cost Sinatra and his backers some $60,000—a considerable sum in the 1940s, but a fraction of the amount that Dorsey would have garnered if he hadn't listened to [Moretti and pals.]"

Wait! One more point about Sinatra: Almost every time I read about him, and sometimes when I hear him sing, I go back in my mind to *The Ed Sullivan Show*, the classic Sunday night TV variety show that lasted from the late forties to the early seventies, for a big laugh. It was when comedian and master of intentional mispronunciation Norm Crosby, speaking about Sinatra, called him Frank Senestra.

KUDOS TO LEROY DIGGS

To lace on a pair of eight-ounce gloves and climb into the squared circle, face to face with a man intent on relieving you of your senses, is to give the world irrefutable proof of your courage before a punch is thrown.

~*John Schulian*
Writers' Fighters & Other Sweet Scientists

In John Schulian's book *Writers' Fighters & Other Sweet Scientists*, which is a compilation of his articles and columns written between 1974 and 1984, he writes about boxing in trenchant and often hilarious fashion. And it isn't an exaggeration to say his observations about fighters and other individuals involved in the sport surge off the page.

For example, in his piece about promoter Don King, clearly not one Schulian's favorite people, he writes about the time King hosted a press luncheon before the October 2, 1980, Holmes vs. Ali title bout. His guests were served ham and cheese sandwiches, the kind of cheap meal, Schulian says, "King prefers when he picks up the tab."

One of the problems King didn't anticipate was, Schulian says, "Muslims don't eat pork and Ali is a Muslim. 'Heh-heh-heh,' said King, nervously flicking the ashes from his cigar." Understandably, Ali was angry "and the Muslims who never leave [his] side seemed to be considering how the well-fed King would look on a spit with an apple in his mouth."

The most interesting chapter in Schulian's book concerns Leroy Diggs, heavyweight champion Larry Holmes's sparring partner for his 1981 title defense against Leon Spinks.

(Diggs was in demand as a sparring partner for such heavyweights as Earnie Shavers, Muhammad Ali, and Spinks.)

Diggs, who was the same size as Holmes, six foot three and 220 pounds, spoke glowingly of the man nicknamed the Easton Assassin, saying, "He gives you your respect."

But Diggs knew the big drawback of being a sparring partner was that after Holmes defeated Spinks by a third round TKO, "nobody will realize that Leroy Diggs had anything to do with it."

Put simply, Diggs and his counterparts aren't given the recognition they deserve. I'm waiting for a fighter, after an important victory, to publicly name his sparring partners and give them credit.

Regarding Diggs's approach to both his job as a sparring partner and his thoughts about Holmes, he told Schulian, "You understand what's your job, so you just get on with it. They tell you to come into camp in shape and you do it. Larry, it don't matter that much to him. He can get in shape as he go along. There's three of us spars with him and we got to get him mean, got to get him being two different people.... You make him miss in the ring and he want to kill you. Don't matter how nice he is when we're sittin' around nights playin' cards. His ass gonna be up for a whippin' when he's fightin' for real, not mine."

After Diggs's days as a sparring mate were over, for a short time he became, Schulian writes, "a small town cop." He learned the job wasn't for him, however, when early one morning he encountered a carload of drunks and, he says, "Your heart be beatin.' You know they're bombed out of their gourds. Mother love, it's all you can do keep yourself from turnin' around and runnin'."

In the last section, "Champions Forever," Schulian pays tribute to Gene Tunney, Jack Dempsey, Jake LaMotta, Johnny Bratton, Archie Moore, Henry Armstrong, and Joe Louis, about whom he writes, "As a fighter and a human being, he had been something that even death won't erase. He was too big for it, just as he was too big for life. The candle is out, but the light still shines."

Memorable line, that last one.

THE OMNIPRESENT DOCTOR SAX AND A BLACK COAT ON A HOOK

Memory and dream are intermixed in this mad universe.

~Jack Kerouac
Dr. Sax

1

In Jack Kerouac's novel *Dr. Sax*, we meet young Jack Duluoz, the author's alter ego, a young boy who has been schooled on *The Shadow* radio program, *The Shadow* magazine, *Weird Tales*, and other radio and magazine frights.

Kerouac's book is a cautionary tale reminding us that in our existence we all had, have, or will have a Dr. Sax with whom to contend. So be on guard for *your* Dr. Sax, reader.

A daunting and mysterious book, *Dr. Sax* was written in 1952 and published in 1959, when the author was thirty years old. Set in industrial Lowell, Massachusetts, in 1938, Kerouac takes us into the powerful and unlimited imagination of young Duluoz, who daily encounters fantasy and reality, and sometimes a mix of both.

True, at times the novel is maddening because of Kerouac's spontaneous prose. Some advice: Stick with it. Use your imagination. Make the book your own. Try to lose yourself in the story's strangeness and the way it's written.

(I promise that you won't be tested on the book.)

2

An example of everyday life's reality, in young Duluoz's active outer world, is his mother who, he writes, "in reality every evening sat out on a chair, one foot inside the house in case the peaked little porch on top of things and wires and with its frail aerial birdlike supports should fall."

Also, another character—a minor one but part of Duluoz's outer world—is Zagg, Pawtucketville's best known drunk. Duluoz tells us he "looked exactly like Hugh Herbert and staggered around saying 'Woo Woo!' because he knew it, but was really drunk—There's Zagg with a mashed cigar in his face protesting with my father about how he won the high score, he bowled 143 and won the high score prize, where was the prize, and my father smiling and saying 'I know Zagg, goddamit, I know you bowled 143 — I seen it in every strike you threw down the gutter...'"

Turning to young Duluoz's vivid inner world, the omnipresent Dr. Sax is its most memorable figure. He "hides around the corner of my mind," Duluoz says. His image is frightening: "[He's] masked by night shadow flitting over the edge of the sandbank.... beneath the bridge, slouching, dark, emitting a high laugh, 'Mwee hee ha ha,' fading, choking, mad maniac, caped, green-faced (a disease of the night) glides Doctor Sax — along the rocks...."

Another key Dr. Sax scene: Early on in the novel Duluoz sees Dr. Sax in his bedroom. While his mother and sister are asleep in the family's large bed, "In darkness in mid-sleep night I saw him standing over my crib with wild hair, my heart stoned, I turned horrified."

3

Here's what a friend told me about *Dr. Sax*, the same friend who recommended the book to me, and he's usually correct when he talks about books.

Friend: I feel a wacky, eerie connection with one of Jack Duluoz's fantasies, you know.

RZ: Connection?

Friend: Well, as soon as I read it, I knew we connected. (Pause) It's when he says: "The underground rumbling horror of the Lowell night—a black coat on a hook on a white door—in the dark—o-o-h!—my heart used to sink at sight, of huge headshroud rearing on the rein in the goop of my door." That's it. The nightmare! The fantasy!

RZ: (Pause) Think you've outgrown it?

Friend: I think I have, yes. But there are times when I think about that black coat hanging there waiting to be filled, and I ask myself by what? When I think about it all these years later, I still shiver. I handle the problem by going somewhere else in my mind.

RZ: Filled by what? That's disturbing! But, old sausage, Duluoz's fear of that black coat hanging there on a hook is a perfect example of his outer and inner merging.

Friend: More like colliding.

RZ: Think of that image of Dr. Sax, in the last chapter, "standing there with his hands in his pockets, his mouth dropped open, uptilted his searching profile into the enigmatic sky—"

Friend: Yes, yes, yes. And "I'll be damned," Dr. Sax says. "The universe disposes of its own evil." He says that because, as he tells Duluoz, the Bird of Paradise has saved mankind and "destroyed the Snake of Evil."

RZ: What an unforgettable scene!

Friend: And then Duluoz tells us he has "seen Dr. Sax several times since, at dusk, in autumn, when the kids jump up and down and scream—he only deals in glee now."

RZ: The way the novel ends—

Friend: On a positive note—that's how. Duluoz finds a flower—right?—puts it in his hair, finds another flower and puts that one in his hair, too. Then he heads home. Life goes on. "By God," are young Jack's last two words in the book.

RZ: That chapter and the earlier one about the Lowell flood contain the book's best writing, because in them Kerouac captured the throb and wildness of the moment, which he did in many of his other books, too. It's Walt Whitman's influence.

Friend: And don't forget the ladies he sees in the last chapter. That image has always stayed with me.

RZ: Yes, y-yes, the ladies. Young Duluoz passes the Grotto again, sees a cross on a rock and the ladies—

Friend: All devout French Canadian ladies praying on their knees. Then he finds another flower and puts it in his hair.

RZ: And, unlike Thomas Wolfe's George Webber, Duluoz goes home again.

EVERYTHING YOU EVER WANTED TO KNOW ABOUT SHAKESPEARE

If the writing is at all interesting... you are imagining the mind behind the prose. Often that imagining takes a direct, even visceral form: who is this person? No matter how discreet or unforthcoming writers may be, they are present, and readers form judgments about them.

~Tracy Kidder and Richard Todd
Good Prose.

Little is known about William Shakespeare's life, especially the early part, but a huge number of books have been written about him, and Peter Ackroyd's readable, carefully researched, and enthusiastically written *Shakespeare: The Biography* is one of them.

(Ackroyd has also authored biographies of Charles Dickens, T.S. Eliot, and William Blake.)

For readers unfamiliar with Shakespeare, Ackroyd doesn't try to intimate or impress them with his knowledge of the bard: Rather he wants them to understand, or begin to understand, Shakespeare.

Consider these five points he makes about Shakespeare:

1. He copied—though borrowed might be a more polite way to put it—from other Elizabethan dramatists, and his rival Christopher Marlowe borrowed from him, which wasn't a big deal back in those days. Shakespeare even went a step further by plagiarizing himself because that was how "his imagination worked," says Ackroyd. (Want proof? Ackroyd suggests looking at *The Two Gentlemen of Verona* and *Romeo and Juliet*, and then *A Midsummer Night's Dream* and *The Tempest*.)

2. As for plots and incidents, Shakespeare had little interest in them. Instead, Ackroyd writes, "His interest lay in reimagining events and characters." Reimagining is key.

3. Shakespeare's memory? Well, it was huge. When he read a book, he always mined something from it for future use.

4. Ambiguity was continuously in the forefront of Shakespeare's mind. Always! Many of his characters have many selves housed in a single self. For example, Ackroyd asks, "Is Henry V a bullying thug or a great leader of men? Is he made of valour or formed from ice or snow?"

5. Shakespeare wrote hurriedly, maybe even carelessly and "sometimes he muddled names, or gave characters different names in the course of a play. Characters are often given different descriptions or professions."

Final two points: First, you should know that Shakespeare — Ackroyd's Shakespeare — isn't much different from us wannabe writers. Second, Shakespeare can be spelled many different ways: S-h-a-k-s-p-e-r, S-h-a-x-p-e-r-e, and S-h-a-c-k-s-p-e-r-e.

I like Shaxpere because the letter **x** always intrigues me.

DUCK! HERE COME THOSE FRIGGIN' BOOK GODS

Tons of emails assaulted me in early May — and I'm not exaggerating. A variety of ads from bookstores (local and otherwise), a private library I never knew existed, Amazon.com, Barnes & Noble, the Library of America, Goodreads, and Books and More Books were among the assailants.

The ads focused on Walt Whitman. Why? May 31, 2019, was the great American poet's two hundredth birthday.

I'm positive the book gods, those mischievous spirits, planned the assault. Once they have you in their sights they're relentless, and they wanted me to pay heed to Mr. Whitman.

The email barrage was their first attack, and it was mild compared to the second one which came shortly afterward on an early June morning. I was at the local library. Two books I had taken out needed returning.

The intelligent part-time librarian was a full-time student at a nearby college and sometimes a full-time smart ass.

> Librarian: Hey, Jack Duluoz! Good to see ya! You know if you still like Jack Kerouac, you might be interested in Walt Whitman. They're both selfish writers.

> RZ: Selfish writers? Surely you jest.

> Librarian: Don't call me Shirley.

> RZ: Ah ha! Loved *Airplane*. Now to business. You know I'm a Kerouac fan. So explain yourself, young man, when you say he and Walt are selfish writers.

> Librarian: They write only about themselves and their experiences, which also means their imaginations are limited. Toss in Henry Miller, too. It's as if — especially with Whitman — no one else in the world exists. Proof? Check out how *Leaves of Grass* begins: "I celebrate myself/ And what I assume you shall assume." Remember that? Later in the poem he does the same thing: "I dream in my dreams all the dreams of other dreamers,/ And I become the others." The guy believes he speaks for everyone.

> RZ: I'm impressed with your memory.

Librarian: I am, too. It's photogenic. I mean photo-
graphic. Many of Kerouac's books, I'm sure you
know, are narrated by Jack Duluoz, his secret
sharer, which means Kerouac is Duluoz and Duluoz is Kerouac, right?

RZ: Autobiographical fiction is what it's called.

Librarian: Anyway, it's Whitman's two billionth
birthday this month and I have a copy, right
here, of a book published in 2019, in honor of his
happy day. I thought of you right away after my
sister gave it to me for my birthday a few days
ago. Take it. It's yours.

So I took it.

And it was worth taking.

Walt Whitman Speaks is a prose compilation of the
poet's views on a variety of issues during an interview in
1888. I was interested in what he said about various writers
and what his philosophy of life was.

On Mark Twain: "I have met Clemens, met him
many years ago, before he was rich and famous. Like all
humorists he was very sober... slow to move, liking to stop
and chat — the kind of fellow one is quietly drawn to."

On Leo Tolstoy: "[He] is a world force — an immense
vehement first energy driving to the fulfillment of a great
purpose."

On Henry David Thoreau: "One thing about Thoreau keeps him very near to me. I refer to his lawlessness —

his dissent—his going his own absolute road let hell blaze all it chooses."

Regarding Whitman's philosophy, he said, "I do not teach a definite philosophy—I have no cocked and primed system—but I outline, suggest, hint—tell what I see—then each may make up the rest for himself."

Sage words.

AT THE MALL

It happened when the Norwichtown Mall existed, probably forty years ago, and Waldenbooks was one of its main attractions. A Tuesday summer evening in July. I was there to buy a few books and spotted several used ones looking lonely and uncomfortable on a neglected table in the corner of the store.

There, to my left, was a copy of Herman Melville's *Moby Dick*—which brought to mind the American Literature class I took in the mid-1960s. One of our assignments was to read and write about Melville's strange book.

The passage I've never forgotten involves that mad bastard Captain Ahab and the time he cried and one of his tears fell into the Pacific Ocean. Well, I opened the used book, which of course had that musty odor old books have. The page didn't matter. Any page would do. Wrong! The page I turned to contained the passage about Ahab's tear.

That was my introduction to the Book Gods, those roguish spirits who intervene in one's life without warning. I have no doubt they made me pick Melville's book. I have no doubt they made me turn to that key moment in Ahab's miserable life.

My bookstore encounter with the Gods stayed with me ever since that long-ago summer evening. I even memorized the passage and when I wanted to impress someone that Ahab had at least one moment of humanity and sanity, despite his insanity, I simply rattled off Melville's words.

And what he wrote—it's in "The Symphony" chapter—was that "from beneath his slouched hat Ahab dropped a tear into the sea; nor did the Pacific contain such wealth as that one weep drop."

But hold on! Hold on because on a September afternoon, about a year later, I showed off to a friend—he knows his Melville, Hawthorne, and Poe—and quoted Melville's words. He told me emphatically I had misquoted Melville and the correct version was this: "... from beneath his slouched hat Ahab dropped a tear into the sea; nor did the Pacific contain such wealth as that one wee drop."

A smug I-told-you-so expression appeared on his face. No surprise. No sense arguing with him, either, and if it makes him happy to believe I misquoted Melville and he got it right, so be it and frick him...

And for those who say the Book Gods don't exist, I say what would we do without them?

BOGIE WITHOUT BACALL

Many film critics, like Alan G. Barbour, have called 1954's *The Barefoot Contessa* a "pretentious soap opera." I disagree. If you like intelligent dialogue, a fine Bogart performance, and noteworthy shifts in point of view, and even pretentious soap operas, the movie doesn't disappoint.

It even has a touch of *film noir*: It begins in the rain and many of the scenes, including a double murder and subsequent suicide, take place at night. Yikes!

The Barefoot Contessa focuses on Ava Gardner's character, Maria Vargas, who begins as a nobody, but thanks to Harry Dawes (Bogart), a screenwriter and director, becomes a famous movie star.

Gardner's beautiful and vulnerable Maria is surrounded by predators, like the wealthy, boorish Kirk Edwards (Warren Stevens), the slick Alberto Bravano (Marius

Goring), and the unbalanced Count Vincenzo Torlato-Favrini (Rossano Brazzi).

Also, there's Edmond O'Brien's character, Oscar Muldoon, who's a stunning example of verbal diarrhea, but to his credit he keeps his distance from Maria.

(For his performance the always reliable O'Brien won the Oscar for the year's Best Supporting Actor. Well deserved.)

Bogart's Dawes has a complex relationship with Maria. During her and the Count's wedding reception, the cynical but decent Dawes approaches the groom and tells him his relationship with Maria has been "a strange one from the start," and that "I've never known what it was really — friend, director, confessor, part-time amateur psychiatrist." He adds, "She's lived her whole life as a fairy tale, you know."

Count Torlato-Favrini: No, I did not know.

Dawes: And she's never been in love before. Take my word for it. She vulnerable. Wide open to be hurt badly. Emotionally she's a child. She's wrapped all her adolescent dreams up in one dream prince and you're it.

Count: That's quite a responsibility.

Dawes: I don't want her hurt badly. I don't want her hurt at all.

Count: You think I do? I don't mind what you've said, Mr. Dawes, but I wonder why did you find it necessary to say it.

Dawes: Oh I don't know. My number six sense again, maybe.

Count: Number six?

Dawes: Another private joke.

On her wedding night Maria learns that several years ago the Count suffered a war wound, rendering him impotent. She believes there's only one way to solve the problem and that's by becoming pregnant by an unnamed lover. Of course the Count learns of her unfaithfulness and shoots her, her lover, and himself.

On screen Bogart's Dawes served as a protector for Gardner's Maria, but their off-screen relationship was a different matter. A well-known tease, Bogart immediately began verbally poking fun at Gardner, which caused her to dislike and mistrust him. Too, she became wary of the movie's Oscar winning director and screenwriter Joseph Mankiewicz, who, when Bogart taunted her in his presence, did nothing to stop it.

A year later Bogart starred with Gene Tierney in *The Left Hand of God*. The actress was "unstable," Jeffrey Meyers writes in *Bogart: A Life in Hollywood*. "She had a retarded child who was placed in an institution and had been incapacitated by several nervous breakdowns."

Bogart recognized Tierney's symptoms because both his third wife Mayo Methot and his sister Pat suffered from illness. "Though usually critical of actors who were unprepared and made mistakes," Meyers writes, "Bogart was as patient with Tierney's mental illness as he had been with [his sister] and [his third wife] and helped her complete the picture."

Tierney praised Bogart, Meyers writes, as "kind and gentle. He was nothing less.... His presence and understanding carried me through the film. We did not know then that he was terminally ill with cancer."

VILLANELLE/EVE

1

I asked a friend to send me a novel set during the paranoia of the Cold War, and he did. Quickly too, because he owns a bookstore.

Killing Eve is the novel's title and its author is Luke Jennings. Its two main characters are M15 security operative Eve Polastri and Oksana Astankova.

(Made into a British TV series, Sandra Oh stars as Eve and Jodie Comer portrays the dangerous, unpredictable Oksana, or Villanelle, her code name. They're perfect.)

At the end of the novel, in a crucial scene that takes place in Eve's apartment, Villanelle — who's such a delicious psychopath — gives Eve advice about staying alive.

> Villanelle: the only way of surviving is if you and I
> work together. You have to put your life in my
> hands, and do exactly, and I mean exactly, what

I say. You have to accept your life here is over. No more marriage, no more flat, no more job. Basically, no more Eve Polastri.

Eve: So—

Villanelle: I take you into my world. I mean the world that's all around you... but which is invisible if you're not part of it. In Russia we call it *mir teney*, the shadow world.

2

Several other key aspects resonate in Jennings's engrossing novel. First, there's Eve's gradual and fascinating realization that "the mystery, and the woman [Villanelle] at the heart of the mystery, speak to a part of [her] that she's never really explored." Eve has become fascinated by that aspect of herself.

Second: "Who is the unnamed woman who has carved such a bloody trail through the shadowlands of the intelligence world?" Jennings writes. "Who are her employers? What do they want? How have they achieved such terrifying power and reach?"

Third—and it's the novel's big reveal— Eve learns she has been *used* by her superiors because she made the mistake of trusting them.

3

At the end of the novel, Eve and Villanelle leave Eve's apartment and disappear together. When they return— and they will—one has to wonder if Eve will still be the smart but bored security operative we met early in the novel, or has she been "transformed into someone who acts as her target does? Who kills without hesitation or pity?" Of Villanelle, she's too unpredictable to hazard any opinions about what she might do. Just be ready for the unexpected!

The most striking sentence in the book is when Villanelle tells Eve about *mir teney*.

ADVENTURES OF
HUCK AND PIC

Beginnings

In Jack Kerouac's novella *Pic* (1971), the main character is ten-year-old Pictorial Review Jackson, while Huck Finn is, of course, Mark Twain's central creation in *Adventures of Huckleberry Finn* (1884).

Their vernacular is similar and believable. Here's how Twain's book begins his novel: "You don't know about me without you have read a book by the name of 'Adventures of Tom Sawyer.' But that ain't no matter. That book was made by Mr. Mark Twain."

And when Huck says, *"There was things which he stretched, but he mainly told the truth,"* well, that's one of my favorite lines in all literature.

Kerouac opens young Pic's story this way: "Ain't never nobody loved me like I love myself, 'cept my mother and she's dead. (My grandfather, he's so old he can remember a hunnerd years back but what happened last week and the day before, he don't know.)

Travels by Land

Pic and his hard working brother Slim hitchhike from rural North Carolina to New York City, where they meet and are welcomed by the admirable Father McGillicuddy, a Jesuit priest. Slim needs a job and the priest hires him and Pic for the weekend. Custodial work.

After Pic sings the Lord's Prayer during a Sunday service, he speaks joyfully to his late grandfather, "Grandpa, I even whistled and I wished I had my harmonica, and the priest man sang up and said I sung up like an angel."

During his travels by land Huck has an experience that scars him for life. It involves his friend Buck Grangerford. After finding his way to the Grangerford residence and being accepted by the family, he and Buck, who's Huck's age, probably twelve or thirteen, become friends. From him Huck learns about the longstanding Grangerford-Shepherdson feud that has claimed the lives of many members of both families.

One morning Huck witnesses Buck and his nineteen- year-old cousin in a gun battle with several Shepherdsons. For safety, Huck climbs a tree and hides in it until dark. When he climbs down, he creeps along the riverbank and discovers, he tells us, "two dead bodies lying in the edge of the water. "

One of them is Buck.

After pulling each body ashore, Huck says, "I covered up their faces, and got away as quick as I could. I cried a little when I was covering up Buck's face, for he was mighty good to me."

Endings

For the damaged Huck what passes for civilization is too much for his young mind and heart to accept. Too much killing. Too much injustice. He wants out! His only recourse is, he tells us, "to light out for the Territory ahead of the rest because Aunt Sally she's going to adopt me and sivilize me and I can't stand it. I been there before."

I been there before. A sad, unforgettable comment from a sad, unforgettable young boy.

Pic ends on a hopeful, gentle note. He and Slim are back at Slim's New York home and the smart, happy Pic says: "And Sheila [Slim's wife] run up, kissed him hungrily, and we went in to eat the steak she saved up for us, with mashy potatoes, pole beans, and cherry banana spoon ice cream split."

A Word about Kerouac

In Kerouac's books his word images of people, places, and things are extraordinary. For me, each time I revisit them they seem changed, a gift of prose magic few writers possess.

Take Kerouac's image of Slim, near the end of the novella, playing his trumpet at Harlem's Pink Cat Club: "He blew in the horn, and moved his poor fingers, and I tell you grandpa he made the purtiest deep down horn-sound like when you hear a big New York City boat way out in the river at night, or like a train, only he made it sing up and down melodious. He made the sound all trembly and sad, and blew so hard his neck shaked all over and the vein popped out in his brow." What Slim does next is "[turn] the horn back to Sheila and [he] finished the song with his head way down on the mouthpiece and the horn against his shoe, and stood like that and bowed."

That kind of writing, robust, vivid, and filled with life, is common in Kerouac's other works. For example, in *On the Road* (1957) a similar passage occurs near the end of the book. Kerouac's main character and narrator, Sal Paradise, is living in Chicago with his friend Dean Moriarty, and one evening they see "a gang of bop musicians" entering a saloon. There's "the leader" who's described by Paradise as "a slender, drooping, curly-haired, pursy-mouthed tenorman, thin of shoulder, draped loose in a sports shirt, cool in the warm night, self-indulgence written in his eyes, who picked up his horn and frowned in it and blew cool and complex and was dainty stamping his foot to catch ideas, and ducked to miss others—and said, 'Blow,' very quietly when the other boys took solos." More, "The third sax was an alto, eighteen-year-old cool, contemplative young Charlie Parker-type Negro from high school, with a broadgash mouth, taller than the rest, grave... He raised his horn and blew into it quietly and thoughtfully and elicited birdlike phrases and architectural Miles Davis logics."

And who were these musicians, these life-affirming artists?

"These were," Paradise says, "the children of the great bop innovators."

RICHIE THE WHIZ

I woke up one May morning—the year was 1948—and turned to the sports page of the New Haven *Journal and Courier*, gazed at the Philadelphia Phillies vs New York Giants box score, and said out loud, "I like the Phillies of Philadelphia and their centerfielder Richie Ashburn will be my favorite player forever, and maybe someday I'll go to Philadelphia and Shibe Park, home of the Phillies, and see a game. Maybe."

No one I knew liked the Phillies and because I'm naturally contrary, I decided to make them my favorite team. Baseball fans in New Haven liked the Yankees, the Giants, or the Dodgers. No other teams seemed to exist.

Why Richie Ashburn? He batted left; so did I. He threw right; so did I. He played centerfield and in those pick-up games at Beaver Pond Park and the Mud Flats, where we thirteen and fourteen-year-olds would play hardball almost daily, I'd station myself in centerfield.

Richie was born in Tilden, Nebraska, wherever that was. I was born in Hamden, Connecticut, and to my mind back then there wasn't really much difference between the two places.

I even tried changing my batting stance so it would resemble Richie's. Disaster.

In 1948, his first year in the majors, Richie batted .333, played in 117 games, and led the National League in stolen bases with 32. He made the National League All-Star team, and against the power-packed American League All-Stars hit two singles, stole a base, and scored a run.

The Sporting News voted him 1948's Rookie of the Year.

In 1958 he won his second National League batting title with a .350 average. He also led the league in hits, triples, walks, and on-base percentage.

During the winter of 1962 he was traded to the New York Mets, at the time the worst team in major league baseball history. Though the Mets only won forty games that season, Richie went out a winner, batting .306 and walloping seven home runs, the most he ever hit during his fifteen-year career, twelve of them with the Phillies.

After his season with the Mets, Richie retired with a lifetime batting average of .308. In 1995 he was inducted into the Baseball Hall of Fame.

After retiring he turned to broadcasting and became the voice of the Phillies. "His charming and folksy Nebraska accent was a comfortable sound to Philadelphians for 35 years," Fran Zimniuch writes in *Richie Ashburn Remembered.*

Richie died on September 9, 1997, at 5:30 a.m., of a heart attack in New York's Grand Hyatt hotel. He was seventy-two years old.

Shortly after his death a memorial service was held at Philadelphia's Memorial Hall. Forty thousand people paid their respects to the man who, Zimniuch writes, "was an institution in Philadelphia — an icon to those who loved baseball."

FIFTY YEARS IN THE FIGHT GAME

I n each of boxing historian Jerry Fitch's books, his passion for and knowledge of the sweet science is clearly evident. Published in 2013 and enhanced by many photographs of Fitch and professional fighters, *50 Years of Fights, Fighters and Friendships* contains twenty-seven superbly written chapters, including one about the great welterweight champion Kid Gavilan, who, along with Ralph "Tiger" Jones and Gaspar Ortega, fought on national television more than any other fighter during the 1950s.

Fitch recalls watching Gavilan—who was born Geraldo Gonzáles on January 26, 1926, in Camaguey, Cuba—his parents' small television set defending his world welterweight title against 1950's television darling Chuck Davey.

The 1953 fight, held at the Chicago Stadium, was nationally televised on the popular *Wednesday Night Fights.*

(Pabst Blue Ribbon beer was the sponsor. What'll you have? Pabst Blue Ribbon!)

After Davey, a southpaw, was floored for the first time in round one of the scheduled fifteen rounder, it became apparent a mismatch was taking place. Though game, Davey was floored three more times in the ninth round and his team wisely refused to let him come out for round ten.

(Before the fight was stopped, Gavilan, nicknamed the Cuban Hawk, hadn't lost a round.)

Twenty-two years later "the great Angelo Dundee gave me [Gavilan's] phone number one day," Fitch writes, "while [he] and Muhammad Ali were in Cleveland promoting the Ali-Wepner fight. Gavilan was apparently part of the Ali camp at this time so he was staying at the same hotel."

Fitch contacted the former welterweight champion and learned he was appearing that afternoon at a nearby karate studio.

"The image I remember most with Kid Gavilan that day had nothing to do with the interview I conducted or with any unique facts I obtained during our conversation," Fitch writes. When Gavilan was announced to the gathering, "everyone stood and began applauding and Gavilan suddenly jumped up and began shadow boxing and throwing bolo punches. From the crowd's reaction I truly believe many in the crowd thought the bolo was a karate move. They roared!"

(Bolo punch? It's a combination hook and uppercut. It's not a punch that would knock out an opponent, though I wouldn't want to be hit by it, nor would you. Instead, it often confused an opponent. Its most recent practitioners were Sugar Ray Leonard, Joe Calzaghe, and Roy Jones Jr.)

Gavilan's professional boxing career began in 1943. In 1953 the Boxing Writers of America named him Fighter of the Year. He retired in 1958 with a 105-30-5 (28 KOs) record.

He was never knocked out and rarely knocked down.

One of the few fighters to drop him was Carmen Basilio. In their September 18, 1953, welterweight title bout at Syracuse's Onondaga County War Memorial, Basilio's perfectly timed left hook to Gavilan's jaw dumped the Cuban Hawk on his tokus in the second round.

Back on his feet at nine, Gavilan realized that slugging with Basilio wasn't the way to fight the 4-1 underdog from Canastota, New York. Deciding to box, not slug with Basilio, he earned a split decision, much to the displeasure of the pro-Basilio crowd.

According to Gary B. Youmans, in *The Onion Picker: Carmen Basilio and Boxing in the 1950s*, after the fight Gavilan said Basilio was much tougher than he had expected, but "I think I beat him easily. After the first knockdown he never did anything else to me."

Ring magazine voted Kid Gavilan the twenty-sixth greatest fighter of the last eighty years.

RICHIE'S PERFECT STRIKE

[Richie Ashburn] was the greatest
defensive outfielder I ever saw.

~Willie Mays

It has been confirmed by a variety of scientific sources too numerous to mention that baseball fans love lists of baseball players. Well, here's a list I compiled and I hope the names on it bring back memories: Del Ennis, Eddie Waitkus, Willie Jones, Granny Hamner, Mike Goliat, Dick Sisler (the great George Sisler's son), Robin Roberts (the greatest pitcher of his era), Russ Meyer, Ken Heintzelman, Bob Miller, Stan Lopata, Curt Simmons, Johnny Blatnik, Hank Borowy, Jack Brittin, Putsy Caballero, Bubba Church, Blix Donnelly, Stan Hollmig, Jack Mayo, Bill Nicholson, Paul Stuffel, Jocko Thompson, Andy Seminick, Dick Whitman, Steve Ridzik, Ken Silvestri, and Richie Ashburn.

And I hope I didn't forget anyone.

If you say, "Hey, they were members of the Phila-delphia Phillies," you're right. Nicknamed the Whiz Kids, those brash young guys fooled many baseball experts and fans by winning the 1950 National League pennant, the franchise's first since 1915.

Some facts about the Whiz Kids: The team's average age was twenty-six... Many of the players had career years... The soft spoken, intelligent Eddie Sawyer, a mere thirty-nine years of age, managed the team... Perhaps the most forgotten Whiz Kid, despite hitting 13 homeruns in 145 games — which back then was respectable — was second baseman Mike Goliat.

Some personal non-facts about the Whiz Kids: Third baseman Willie Jones, nicknamed Puddin' Head, had one of professional baseball's greatest nicknames... Half the season was over before I realized Granny Hamner's last name wasn't Hammer... As for the team's size, I thought each player was five foot ten and weighed 170 pounds.

~~

The first week in October 1950, at Ebbets Field, Brooklyn, was when Richie Ashburn's alertness saved the game for the Phillies.

In the September 10, 1990, edition of the *Philadelphia News*, Ashburn explained the events of that afternoon in his weekly column: "[Duke] Snider lined a hard single to cen-terfield. I charged the ball and threw a perfect strike to Stan Lopata, and Cal Abrams was out by 10 feet. The truth is, I had shortened my position in centerfield a few steps as every outfielder would do with the winning run on second base in the bottom of the ninth.

"Snider hit a bullet, a perfect one-hopper; and all I had to do was get off a decent throw to home. To be accurate, it was a fairly routine play executed perfectly in a very crucial situation."

If third base coach "Milt Stock had held [Abrams on third base after Snider's single], the Dodgers would have had the bases loaded and nobody out, and [Robin] Roberts would have had to pitch to [Jackie] Robinson, the best clutch hitter in a lineup of great hitters."

In the top of the tenth, with the score tied 1-1, Dick Sisler belted a towering three-run homer, putting the Whiz Kids ahead 4-1. Vying for his twentieth win of the season, Roberts, in the bottom of the tenth, pitched a three up, three down inning.

The 47th World Series would be played between the National League champion Philadelphia Phillies and the American League champion New York Yankees.

THE RING RETIRES

I hope [readers] smile, frown, laugh and cry, as they realize what this incredible artifact represents. When they finish the book... I hope they conclude [that] there was no better portrait of a sport in our society than the (New York) City Ring, and there never will be.

~Mark Allen Baker
Between the Ropes at Madison Square Garden

What prompted the award-winning, prolific Mark Allen Baker to write his latest book, the solidly researched and enthusiastically written *Between the Ropes at Madison Square Garden: The History of an Iconic Boxing Ring, 1925-2007*, was, he said, "an announcement by Madison Square Garden and my affiliation with the International Boxing Hall of Fame. When MSG announced they were retiring one of its most treasured artifacts, a boxing ring, and donating it to the International Boxing Hall of Fame in Canastota, New York, it was beyond belief."

Baker knew he had a story to tell about the boxing ring and "the incredible history that took place atop its canvas.... No other table of humanity offered so much opportunity or destroyed so many dreams quicker."

Miceli and Others

In his book, Baker writes about fighters who have fought in the Madison Square Garden ring, including Syracuse's Joey DeJohn and Brooklyn's Joe Miceli, two of my favorites, and the tragic Billy Bello and the great Roy Jones, Jr.

The unpredictable, hard punching DeJohn slugged it out with Pete Mead at the Garden on February 25, 1949. Dropped twice and taking a beating for six rounds, Mead stormed back in the seventh round, "livid over the beating he had endured," Baker writes. "He became transfixed at returning it to DeJohn and he did just that."

After DeJohn was dropped for the third time in the round, referee Johnny Weber stopped the fight, which "*Ring* magazine recognized as one of the ten greatest fights of the 20th century."

Joe Miceli, who began fighting in 1948 and retired in 1961, fought the best lightweights, welterweights, and middleweights of his time. At least forty of his opponents are recognizable by longtime boxing fans. Many were world champions.

Miceli's most notable weapon, a left hook/uppercut delivered rapidly, was an odd but effective punch that took his opponents by surprise.

Though the popular Miceli was a top ten welter-weight from 1950 to 1956 and fought thirty-seven times on television, he never fought for a world title. Why? Too dangerous, too savvy, that's why.

In *New York City's Greatest Boxers*, Jose Corpas writes, "Miceli of New York's Little Italy section... was known as an offensive fighter, but he knew how to duck a punch as well.... What he did not know how to duck were other fighters." So true!

Billy Bello fought Gaspar Ortega at the Garden and was a highly regarded welterweight prospect. The 1963 na-tionally televised fight went ten rounds and Ortega, who was Bello's idol when the New York fighter was a young-ster, earned a split decision.

"For Bello," Baker writes, "it was a bitter loss that was magnified by the press. Many of Bello's mistakes were due to inexperience. Ortega had over one hundred profes-sional fights and by this point in his career wasn't prone to error."

Fourteen days after his loss to Ortega, the twenty-year-old Bello was "found lifeless in the fifth-floor hallway of a Bronx hallway. Near his body were envelopes that contained narcotics and an examination revealed needle marks on his left forearm."

Only the second light heavyweight champion to win a heavyweight title, Roy Jones, Jr. was also "the first former world middleweight champion since Bob Fitzsimmons in 1897 to conquer a heavyweight title."

Jones began fighting professionally in 1989 and the only fighter to defeat him was Montel Griffin in 1997, and that was by disqualification. In 2004, when he fought Antonio Tarver, whom he had already beaten, he was stopped in the second round. Four months later veteran Glen Johnson knocked him out in the ninth round. In 2005 he lost again to Tarver, this time by unanimous decision.

From 2006 to 2008 the once dominant Jones won three fights, but later in the year, when he fought the talented, undefeated Joe Calzaghe at the Garden, he lost a unanimous decision.

He fought twice in 2009, but in his third fight in December he was stopped by Dave Boy Green. In 2010 Bernard Hopkins decisioned him. A year later Russian cruiserweight Denis Lebedev stopped him.

According to boxrec.com, after the Lebedev setback Jones won thirteen of fourteen fights. In 2018, after defeating Scott Sigmon at the Civic Center in Pensacola, Florida, he retired.

In Jones's prime, Baker says, "If there was anything [he] couldn't do, nobody told him."

Diversity

In the superbly crafted, informative *Between the Ropes at Madison Square Garden,* Baker writes that the MSG ring—which he calls "the City Ring"—stands as "an iconic symbol of the Twentieth Century and a portrait of our culture. It has been at the epicenter of [the sport] since John L. Sullivan defended his heavyweight title at the original Garden in 1883." The ring was "a historic artifact" that "has symbolized every element of society imaginable—age, gender, physicality, [and illustrates] the ethnic diversity of the sport."

WHEN ANNE BECAME GITTEL

Born Anna Marie Louisa Italiano on September 17, 1931, she's better known as Academy Award winning actor Anne Bancroft. Why the name change? Well, the bigwigs at Twentieth Century Fox thought her real name was too ethnic.

By 1959, after fifteen dismissible movies, her acting career had stalled, and she returned to New York to reevaluate her profession and work with the highly regarded Vienna-born acting teacher Herbert Berghof, whose future students, Douglass K. Daniel writes in *Anne Bancroft: A Life*, "would include Al Pacino, Robert De Niro, and Matthew Broderick."

Berghof's method, Daniel writes, "drew from the theories of the Russian actor Konstantin Stanislavski, who believed [and taught Anne] that an actor should connect his own feelings to a character and develop an understanding of the character's motivations."

Anne studied her sister Joan, whose emotional life was, she believed, similar to the character she hoped to portray on Broadway in William Gibson's *Two for the Seesaw*, which Fred Coe would produce and Arthur Penn direct.

Gittel Mosca was the character's name.

When she arrived at Coe's office for a meeting in late August 1959, she was already in character. As she chatted with his secretary, she took off her shoe and "made a point to start scratching her foot as he opened the door to greet her, and then naively picked up her shoe to follow him inside," Daniel writes.

Why? Because that's what Gittel would do.

Inside Coe's office she said to him, "Where's the John? I gotta go bad" — which Gittel would say.

Coe had seen enough. The young lady in his office *was* Gittel Mosca.

A week later Anne met Gibson. "My mind blinked," Gibson said. "She could have walked off my pages. Fred called in an actor for her to read with, and she read excitingly, with the exact turns of voice — this was eerie — I had heard when writing the lines and not heard since; I felt we had fallen into a diamond-in-the-rough mine. She dug the lingo that I had written for Gittel."

Two for the Seesaw opened October 19, 1959, in New York, at the Booth Theater. It was Anne's first Broadway appearance. In the two-character play her co-star was the popular veteran stage and film actor Henry Fonda.

The play and Anne's performance were successful. "If Fonda was the old standby at work," Daniel writes, "Anne was the discovery of the season in the eyes of the critics."

After *Seesaw*'s success on Broadway, Anne acted in eleven plays, including *The Miracle Worker* (1959), *The Skin of Our Teeth* (1966), and *Golda* (1975). From 1962 to 2008 she appeared in thirty-seven movies, including the film version of *The Miracle Worker, The Graduate, Silent Movie, The Turning Point, Garbo Talks,* and *To Be or Not to Be.*

For her work in *The Miracle Worker* she received 1962's Best Actress Oscar. Though Anne didn't attend the Oscar ceremony, Joan Crawford stood in for her and read her twenty-two word acceptance speech: "Here's my little speech, dear Joan. There are three reasons why I deserve this award: Arthur Penn, Bill Gibson, and Fred Coe."

MAX THE MAGNIFICO

1

In Ron Howard's film *Cinderella Man* (2005), Max Baer is depicted as a loud-mouth womanizer unremorseful about the death of one of his opponent in 1930.

Howard, along with everyone else involved in making the film, is wrong.

Read boxing historian Colleen Aycock's latest book, *Max Baer: The Life of Heavyweight Champion and Film Star*, because she sets the record straight about the hard-hitting former heavyweight champion.

"Early in his boxing career he killed a man in the ring named Frankie Campbell," Aycock explains. "The story gave Max a 'killer image' and that's what Hollywood came looking for: A good looking man—he was beautiful—who could pass a screen test and who had a reputation as a killer."

In real life he was a fun-loving, kind, and generous man.

"Most people don't know that after Frankie Campbell's death Max was," Aycock writes, "an emotional wreck. It was a personal battle he would fight for the rest of his life."

Actually, Baer's killer image began fifty-one years before *Cinderella Man*'s release. In *The Harder They Fall* he was portrayed as merciless in battering and winning the world heavyweight championship from Primo Carnera, whom he knocked down eleven times, though sources differ on how many times Carnera was floored.

"Nine days after the fight," Aycock writes, "Primo was still recovering in the Columbus Hospital in New York with a broken ankle, and both Buddy [Max's brother] and Max visited him. Max grinned and they shook hands." Then, Aycock continues, "Max whispered in Primo's ear that he had guaranteed payment for his hospital stay."

2

Aycock's book contains eighteen chapters, among them "The Screwball Championship Fight, Tony Galento." Known for his dirty tactics, the man nicknamed "Two Ton" didn't disappoint his fans against Max Baer in their fight at Roosevelt Stadium in New Jersey on July 2, 1940. Low blows, head butting, and eye gouging were some of the tactics he used, but he wasn't successful: Baer was too strong and savvy for "Two Ton."

Comeuppance time had arrived for Galento.

Aycock quotes Gayle Talbot of the *Asbury Park* press: "The fat old tavern keeper was sitting on his stool blowing blood like a harpooned whale. When the bell rang to start the eighth round, his handlers wouldn't let him go out. The only thing the fight proved was that there isn't a heavyweight in the world today worthy of challenging Joe Louis for the championship."

3

Aycock says *The Magnificent Max Baer* is her "heart book" because "it represents my connection to boxing through my father, Ike, a professional boxer during the Great Depression. Abandoned as a teenager in South Texas, my father tried continuing his high school education while working for a dairy for room and board. There was a time in the 30s when a town's entertainment was a makeshift boxing ring where men could throw pennies and nickels on the canvas to encourage a challenge. My father stepped into the ring as a young man so he could buy a pair of shoes."

In 1934 Baer advertised for sparring partners, and Aycock's father traveled to the fighter's training camp in California to help him prepare for his next fight. Like many people who became acquainted with Baer, Ike Aycock came to like and respect him.

A final word. I hope a feature length movie or documentary will be made about the *real life* Max Baer who Aycock astutely writes about in her excellent book. With the right people in charge of such a project, it would make memorable and informative viewing.

RICHIE'S AND YOGI 'S *ISMS*

Before I read Fran Zimniuch's book *Richie Ashburn Remembered,* I knew little about the author, except that he wrote *Phillies: Where Have You Gone?* After reading his book about Ashburn (1927-1997), the great Philadelphia Phillies Hall of Famer and radio announcer for thirty-five years, I was hooked. Zimniuch is a sports journalist readers will enjoy and find informative and knowledgeable.

One aspect of his book deals with Richie's humorous Ashburn-isms. Yes, the great catcher Yogi Berra of the New York Yankees had his Yogi-isms, but let's start with several of Richie's. Enjoy!

You're on, Richie: *[Houston] is the only town where women wear insect repellent instead of perfume... In my 15 years of eligibility [for the Hall of Fame], my center field opposition consisted of Willie Mays, Duke Snider and Mickey Mantle. Hard to believe I didn't make it against those turkeys... I wish I'd known early what I learned late... To cure a batting slump I took my bat to bed with me. I wanted to know my bat a little better... In fact, when I was playing and going well with a certain bat, I would not trust leaving it around or in the dugout. I used to take it to my room and go to bed with it. In fact, I've been in bed with a lot of old bats in my day.*

Okay, Yogi, your turn: *Half the lies they tell about me aren't true... Ninety percent of this game is half mental... The future ain't what it used to be... A nickel ain't worth a dime anymore... It gets late early around here... Never answer an anonymous letter... You can observe a lot by just watching... Always go to other people's funerals, otherwise they won't come to yours... We have deep depth... Pair up in threes... Never say never.*

The Ashburn-isms and Yogi-isms prompted me to read the book Berra wrote with Tom Horton, *It Ain't Over*. In the section titled "Childhood," we're told his parents, Pietro and Paulina, were hard-working and patriotic Italian immigrants who settled in St. Louis and had five children.

One of their grandsons, Yogi's son Dale, played in the majors for the Pittsburgh Pirates and toward the end of his career the New York Yankees. "I was his manager," Yogi writes. The legendary Connie Mack, who owned and managed the Philadelphia Athletics for fifty-three years, "at that time was the only other dad to manage his own son."

Speaking of Mack, Yogi never forgot that after the 1947 World Series between the Brooklyn Dodgers and the Bronx Bombers, the A's manager said, "I have never seen worse catching." Yogi added that Mack also said his team "was going to run us to death the next year. It did not make for a restful winter."

A rookie at the time, Yogi was bothered by Mack's words, but "to be knocked by the great Connie made me work a little bit harder. It also made me a little bit more important. You don't talk about the guy who can't hurt you."

Despite his knowledge of baseball, Mack should've kept his mouth closed. As Yogi put it: "It may not be a great idea to give a twenty-two-year-old catcher with a lot of incentive any more desire by saying we are going to run you off the field next year."

THANKS, MARLON, AND YOU DIDN'T EVEN KNOW ME

As a junior at Hillhouse High School in New Haven, aka the Elm City, I was an underachiever. For the third marking period—the year was 1954—I was moved from a class of twenty-four students to a much smaller one—I think there were eleven in the group—who, like me, didn't care about grades because we just didn't care.

Take note: We weren't troublemakers. Sent to the office? Not often.

Well, once in my case. My English teacher, who looked as if she had escaped from Madame Tussaud's wax museum, read something I wrote in class—which I thought was humorous, but she didn't. She was positive I was loony and sent me to Mr. Penington's office, the school's well-liked assistant principal.

After reading my paper, he smiled and said, "Sit here. When the bell rings, go to your next class."

In the new group the boys sat together and Zelda, the only girl, sat by herself in the back of the class. Tough? Don't get her angry. Terrific softball and basketball player. Most of us were jealous of her because she made it a point to flex her muscles in our direction when she wore short sleeves.

The teacher was Miss Trevor or Travis. (Remember: we're talking sixty-six years ago.) Always neatly attired, maybe in her mid-thirties, I immediately liked her because on the first day of class she didn't say, "I know your reputations. You're lazy students. You won't get away with that with me." Instead, she simply treated us as students who had brains.

Near the end of the marking period our big assignment was to memorize a famous speech. We were to meet in the school auditorium, instead of our usual classroom, and deliver on stage our speech to our classmates.

I picked something from Shakespeare—Mark Antony's "Friends, Romans, and Countrymen" oration—because a few weeks before the assignment, I had seen Marlon Brando as Antony in *Julius Caesar* at the Loew's Poli Theatre in downtown New Haven, and his delivery of that speech, a mix of defiance, honesty, and anger, stayed with me. Motivated me!

I'm not kidding when I say at home, when I was rehearsing Antony's speech to the Romans, I became the great Brando, at the time the hottest actor on the big screen.

Did I understand *Julius Caesar* the tragedy? What it meant? A little bit, I guess, though when I was older I understood it much better.

"Anyone want to volunteer?" asked Miss Trevor or Travis, when we were all seated in the auditorium.

Ah! There's cool Vinnie DeMaio, nicknamed Real Cool. Combing his hair. Big wave in front. Every hair in place. Reminded me of Dion DiMucci, lead singer of Dion and the Belmonts. Wonder which speech Vinnie memorized? Maybe one about how to be very, very cool in high school. Where have you gone, Vinnie DeMaio?

A voice went off in my head—POW!—and interrupted my thoughts of Vinnie: *Get the blasted speech over with!*

VOLUNTEER!

And there I was on stage, standing and shaking behind the podium, first looking at my male classmates and then at Zelda. And they were looking at me!

Suddenly a switch went on somewhere inside me and without any problem I became Brando, who in the movie became Antony, and there I was standing before those unruly Romans, who were my classmates a few seconds ago.

We, Brando and I, began slowly. With expression. No shouting. "Friends, Romans, countrymen... lend me your ears."

And yes, we goofed once. We said, "Whose ransoms did the general coffins fill." We should've said, "Whose ransoms did the general coffers fill."

So what? We plugged on.

The truth is Brando and I, in all modesty, were terrific — especially when we intoned, "When the poor have cried, Caesar hath wept; / Ambition should be made of sterner stuff. / Yet Brutus says he was ambitious, / And Brutus was an honorable man."

(And we really put heft into the words *honorable man!*)

We approached the finish line. Backing slightly away from the podium, we said, "Bear with me; / My heart is in the coffin there with Caesar, / And I must pause till it come back to me."

Shaken with emotion, we pronounced pause *pau-pause*. We stuttered. Deliberately. And yes, facially we expressed our sadness. But there were no tears when we finished the speech, which meant I was me again (not Brando) and I'm in the Hill House High School auditorium, and it's the twentieth century, not 44 BC.

The boys clapped. (Sal DeGaudio, signifying his approval, gave the Worster Street hoot.) I saw Zelda and she nodded — yes, she did — and brought her palms together three times, then flexed a right arm muscle at me and grinned.

And Miss Trevor or Travis, she smiled a "good job" smile at me.

The Antony speech, along with the essays we had been assigned to write for the class, earned me for the marking period a B+ (as in Brando plus). Only fitting!

THEY WERE UNSUNG

Memories

T he *Whiz Kids Take the Pennant: 1950 Philadelphia Phillies* is a terrific book and brought back many memories for this longtime Philadelphia Phillies fan. Edited by Paul Rogers and Bill Nowlin, it's a collection of writings about each Whiz Kid and also includes articles on the team's manager, coaches, owner, broadcasters, and the team's ten greatest games of that pennant-winning season, a season that was, Rogers writes, "epic."

Though Jocko Thompson, Dick Whitman, Milo Candini, and Mike Goliat were four Whiz Kids who weren't as well-known as Richie Ashburn, Robin Roberts, Eddie Waitkus, Granny Hamner, Del Ennis, and Jim Konstanty, they were certainly contributors to the team's first pennant in thirty-five years.

Veteran Presences

The Phillies' average age was twenty-six, and both thirty-nine-year-old manager Eddie Sawyer and team owner and president Robert Carpenter knew before the 1950 season began that several veteran presences were needed to keep things in perspective for the team's youngsters. Pitcher Thompson, outfielder Whitman, and pitcher Candini were among the veterans the Phillies signed.

Thompson's major league baseball career began in 1948, when he was thirty-one years old, and lasted four years. During his career he posted a 6-11 record, appearing in forty-one major league games, all with Philadelphia.

In 1950 he pitched two games for the Whiz Kids, but more important than his stint with them was his military record in World War II. "Thompson was awarded a number of medals and commendations, including two purple hearts (for wounds), a Bronze Star, and a Silver Star," Clayton Truton writes in *The Whiz Kids Take the Pennant.* "His wartime heroics certainly interrupted his baseball career, but his service to his country and to the people of Western Europe left a legacy that lasted long after his days as a professional ballplayer."

Dick Whitman began his major league career with the Brooklyn Dodgers in 1946, and was sold to the Phillies in 1950. Like Thompson, he was a highly decorated World War II veteran, specifically, the recipient of the Bronze Star the Purple Heart, and three battle citations.

During the 1950 season, Whitman appeared in seventy-five games. Though he batted .250, he led the National League in pinch hits with twelve. (His batting average as a pinch hitter was .308.)

Born Mario Milo Candini to hard-working, patriotic immigrant parents in 1917, he suffered from elbow, shoulder, and arm pain during a twenty-year professional baseball career.

From 1943 to 1949 Candini pitched for the Washington Senators and joined the Whiz Kids in 1950. He appeared in eighteen games and posted a 1-0 record, which didn't stop him from asking for a pay raise for the 1951 season. After the 1950 campaign, according to Gregory H. Wolf's piece in *The Whiz Kids Take the Pennant*, he met with team owner Bob Carpenter and told him, "We couldn't have won the pennant without me."

Carpenter liked his logic and signed him for the 1951 season, where he appeared in fifteen games, again winning, you guessed it, one game.

Batting Eighth

Mike Goliat, the Phillies' young second baseman, is usually overlooked when people discuss the 1950 Whiz Kids. In Paul Rogers' article in *The Whiz Kids Take the Pennant*, he writes that Goliat "was a solid-fielding second baseman (a position he had not played in the minor leagues) who started 145 games for those Phillies. He only hit .234, but it was a hard .234 as he slugged 13 home runs and drove in 64 runs, mostly from the eighth spot in the order. Many of his hits were in the clutch. "

In 1951 many baseball scribes and fans predicted the Phillies would be a solid contender for the National League pennant, but by June the pennant-winning team of 1950 was mired in seventh place.

According to Rogers, "Carpenter called all the start-ers to find out what was wrong with the team." When he and Goliat met, the second baseman told the owner, "I'm not the manager, so I'm not telling you what's wrong," adding if Carpenter didn't like his response "he knew what he could do with it."

That was the end of Goliat's career with the Phillies: Off he went to the American League St. Louis Browns.

THAT'S NOT LAURA

"You can't get rid of your own personality. It's going to come through, no matter what you're doing. It's not difficult for me to hide emotion, since I've always hidden it in my personal life."

~Dana Andrews

In most movies of the forties and fifties, the baddie almost always gets his or her comeuppance. Nineteen forty-four's *Laura* is no exception, thanks at the end of the film to a tough, hard boiled homicide detective and another detective's sharp shooting.

In *Laura*, Gene Tierney plays the manipulating, vivacious Laura Hunt, who everyone thinks has been shotgunned to death in her apartment, though what's left of her face is beyond recognition.

Investigating the murder is police detective Mark McPherson (Dana Andrews), who's never without a cigarette dangling from his mouth. His problem is that the more he investigates Laura's homicide, the more he becomes obsessed with her, which is as unhealthy as smoking cigarettes.

There's snobby, acerbic, effeminate gossip columnist Waldo Lydecker (Clifton Webb, in an unforgettable screen debut). Not only does he want to love Laura but, above all, control her.

There's unctuous southerner Shelby Carpenter (Vincent Price), who has an unhealthy relationship with wealthy pretentious socialite Ann Treadwell (Judith Anderson), who's old enough to be his mother. Maybe even his grandmother.

Of their relationship, she says, "He's not good, but he's what I want. We belong together because we're both weak and can't seem to help it."

Director Otto Preminger's film is peopled with deviants! That's right! And that even includes Laura's dedicated maid Bessie Clarey (Dorothy Adams), whose attachment to her employer is more than loyalty. It's a fixation.

Wait! On second thought there's one "character" who, though normal, is never seen. I'm referring to "Laura," Johnny Mercer and David Raksin's haunting theme song. Heard throughout the movie, it has become a classic.

The movie's best lines belong to Webb's Lydecker. Early on, when McPherson asks him if he was in love with Laura, he replies, "Laura considered me the wisest, wittiest, most interesting man she ever met. I was in complete accord with her on that point."

Consider this one: Lydecker tells McPherson he has tried to become kind and gentle and sympathetic. When the detective asks if he has had any success, Lydecker says, "Let me put it this way. I shall be sincerely sorry to see my neighbor's children devoured by wolves."

Two more: First, Lydecker can't resist saying to McPherson, who can't stop playing with one of those little puzzles, the object being to roll ball bearings into small holes, "Something you confiscated in a raid on a kindergarten?" Second, later in the film Lydecker and McPherson are in Laura's apartment and the columnist, aware of the detective's obsession with her, utters his most unforgettable line: "You better watch out, McPherson, or you'll end up in a psychiatric ward. I don't think they ever had a patient who fell in love with a corpse."

The best version of the *Laura* theme song is Ella Fitzgerald's.

MAGGIE AND THE RELAYS

Jack Dulouz, a high school student smitten with classmate Maggie Cassidy, is the main character and narrator of Jack Kerouac's nostalgic novel *Maggie Cassidy*.

The year is 1938 and one evening, in their Lowell,
Massachusetts home, Jack's mother tells him that Maggie is
toying with his emotions, and that she's possessive and
spoiled and Jack should stop seeing her! But Jack, the author's alter ego, doesn't heed mom's advice.

Pauline Cole, another classmate, is the young lady
who's equally as enamored with Jack as he is with Maggie,
Unfortunately, he doesn't pay her the attention she deserves because, well, he's obsessed with Maggie, who he
describes this way: " — the white flesh and the sullen unbe-
lievable river eyes more beautiful than the eyes of all the
sun-eyed blondes of MGM, Scandinavia and the Western
World — The milk of the brow, the pear of the face — "

In the last chapter three years have passed and Jack isn't the narrator. Now we're hearing an all-wise, all-seeing third person voice, who tells us it's two o'clock on a snowy morning and Jack and Maggie, who haven't seen each other for a long time, are traveling along Massachusetts Avenue, and not surprisingly their date didn't go well.

"She laughed in his face," the narrator says, "he slammed door shut [and] drove her home, drove the car back skittering crazily in the slush, cursing."

He should've listened to his mom those many years ago, because French Catholic mothers are rarely wrong!

Matching the nostalgic story of Jack's romance with Maggie is his athletic ability: He's a runner and a good one. So to the Boston Garden Kerouac takes us, to the seaboard relays, in the early evening.

Keep this in mind: Kerouac's writing is often free of the rules/restraints of conventionally written English. (He called it "spontaneous prose; Truman Capote, one of his critics, said it was "typing.") Kerouac read Walt Whitman and learned, as the great American poet said, "to write in the gush, the throb, the flood, of the moment—to put things down without deliberation—without worrying about their style—without waiting for a fit time or place."

Here's an example: "I'd run a mad race against Jimmy Spindros of Lowell and others running for St. John Prep," Jack says. "The Chief they called Spindros, whose great hawk nose had made him stand in bleak fogs of old football games helmet under arm as captain of the Lowell team—long, tall, strong Greek champion of them all who died in the huge glooms of Iwo Jima."

Here's more: "On the cork track of Boston Garden I in my little nail spikes took off with the same luck-jump off the imminent gun bang and flew around the banked turn in my own white lane as fast as I'd ever run in any 30-yard dash and got inside them (the three college runners) on the turn-in lane, probably illegal, behind me I heard them streaking right in my neck but I am flying and hold myself ready to bank into the far turn and wail right around on those nails throwing popcorks at the generation and coming off the broad turn to hand my stick to Mickey Maguire."

Yes, Mickey Maguire who, we learn early in the novel, knew of Jack and Maggie's romance, as did everyone else in their high school.

Maggie... Maggie... Maggie... After handing off the stick to Maguire, who "had to sail off and pound his way around the mad track," Jack's thoughts turn to Maggie and the night in March, not long ago, "by the radiator... she'd started huffing and puffing against me unmistakably... and I didn't know what to do, no idea in my dull crowded-up-with-worlds brain..."

INDUCTED

Nonember 9, at the Mohegan Sun Casino in Uncasville, Connecticut, was an unforgettable evening for the family and friends of New Haven featherweight/ lightweight Eddie Compo. Along with Arturo Gatti, Chad Dawson, Delvin Rodriguez, Teddy "Red Top" Davis, and referee Arthur Mercante Sr., Compo was inducted into the 2019 Connecticut Boxing Hall of Fame.

Another inductee was Sherman Cain. A sportswriter for forty years for the *Journal Inquirer* in Manchester, Connecticut, Cain was the recipient of the George Smith Contribution to Boxing Award.

Longtime boxing judge Don Trella introduced Felix DelGiudice, Compo's nephew, a decorated Korean War veteran, who accepted the award on behalf of the New Haven fighter.

Compo's first professional fight was in 1944 and his last in 1955. During his career he compiled an impressive

75-10-4 record, fighting some of the best featherweights and lightweights of his era, among them Willie Pep, Davis, Tommy Collins, Phil Terranova, Pat Marcune, Paolo Rosi, Julie Kogon, and Chico Vejar.

At the end of his career, he lost five of his last eleven fights.

The winner of fifty-seven of sixty-one fights, Eddie was twenty years old when in 1949, at Waterbury's Municipal Stadium, Willie Pep, the world featherweight champion and one of boxing's greatest defensive fighters, stopped him before 10,722 fans.

At the time Pep's record was 141-2-1 and nobody was beating him, except the great Sandy Saddler.

(Back then Saddler was beating everyone he fought.)

According to Joseph Nichols of the *New York Times*, "Compo performed creditably in the fourth, landing several rights to [Pep's] face." But in round five Pep came back to drop Compo twice.

In round seven "things were going so badly for Compo," Nichols writes, "that one of the seconds in the challenger's corner urged referee Billy Conway to stop it." After being dropped for the third time in the fight, Compo was on his feet when Conway wisely halted the contest at forty-one seconds of the round.

Despite the loss, as Richard D. Biondi and Salvatore A. Zarra write in their excellent book *Elm City Italians: The*

Italian American Prizefighters from New Haven, Connecticut, "Eddie was far from a spent fighter." After Compo's loss to Pep he recorded eleven wins in thirteen fights.

His most important victory during that stretch was an upset of Stamford, Connecticut's Chico Vejar, a 2006 CBHOF inductee, at Madison Square Garden, in 1951.

(Biondi and Zarra point out that "early in his career Vejar fought under the name of Chico Avalos so that his dad wouldn't know he was boxing.")

The loss was Vejar's first in thirty-two bouts. The verdict was split, with judges Jack Sullivan and Bert Grant voting for Compo and referee Teddy Martin backing Vejar, who outweighed Compo by four pounds, 138 to 134.

"Unaccustomed to the ten round distance and facing his most dangerous foeman," the *New York Times* reported, "Vejar fought a characteristic battle, expecting his punching power to claim another victim." His fight plan was wrong because "Compo's experience told the tale."

"After boxing," Biondi and Zarra write, "Eddie worked in the Elm City area as a liquor salesman, an iron-worker, and for the city. Later in life, he refereed fights in Florida and he helped to train his nephew. Eddie and his wife had one child named Edward Jr."

Compo died on January 3, 1998, in Palm Beach, Florida.

SAVED BY BRAD

Character actor Brad Dexter's most memorable movies were *The Magnificent Seven, The George Raft Story, Von Ryan's Express, None but the Brave, The Asphalt Jungle, 99 River Street,* and *Winter Kills.* After he retired from acting, he became a film producer.

More important: He saved Frank Sinatra's life.

Dexter had a role in the 1965 Sinatra-directed *None but the Brave,* which was filmed in Kauai, Hawaii. One morning Sinatra and the wife of the film's executive producer, Ruth Koch, were swimming.

"They had swum out too far," David Lehman writes in *Sinatra's Century: One Hundred Notes on the Man and His World.* "They were fighting a losing battle with the waves," and certain they were going to drown. "Dexter swam out and saved them both. Stretched out on the sand, Sinatra had lost consciousness, and Dexter gave him artificial respiration."

That night Dexter visited Sinatra. "My family thanks you," the singer said to him. The remark struck Dexter as strange, and Lehman quotes him as saying, "[It was] almost as if I had put him in the uncomfortable position of having to thank me for saving his life."

Lehman writes, "Sinatra now associated Dexter with an incident in which he did not necessarily behave with great courage; Dexter had witnessed his moment of weakness."

(After Rat Packer Joey Bishop heard about Sinatra's near-drowning, Lehman writes, he "sent Frank a cable. 'Did you forget yourself? You could have walked on the waves.'")

Time passed and Dexter's relationship with Sinatra continued to deteriorate. When someone mentioned Dexter's name to Sinatra, according to Lehman, the singer would say, "Brad who?" Finally, during the making of 1967's *The Naked Runner*, which starred Sinatra and Dexter produced, they had a face-to-face falling out.

~

Brad Dexter's performance in *99 River Street* (1953) is powerful and convincing, largely because he created the illusion of being on screen much more than he actually was. Splendid work by an actor who deserved more praise during his career than he was given.

Directed by Phil Karlson, *99 River Street* was Dexter's best movie. Its leads were played by John Payne as Ernie Driscoll, a former professional heavyweight prizefighter now eking out a living as a New York City cab driver, and Evelyn Keyes, one of filmdom's most underappreciated actors, as aspiring actress Linda James, one of the few people Ernie trusts.

Add the tantalizing Peggie Castle to the cast, in a supporting role, as Ernie's shrewish wife Pauline. One of her many complaints about Ernie is she could've been a star if she hadn't married him. What a charmer!

Ernie's marriage is shattered after he learns Pauline is having an affair with Dexter's character, the sinister Victor Rawlins, a suave, well-dressed, small-time hood who masterminded a recent jewel robbery.

(In this movie Dexter rivals Richard Conte as one of filmdom's best dressed villains.)

Though it lasts a few minutes, Dexter's best scene takes place in Pauline and Ernie's apartment. That's where he murders her because she has hindered his chance to sell the stolen jewels. They're alone and he tells her to "take it easy, baby." Then stepping behind her, he gently wraps a scarf around her neck.

"Don't," she says, uncertain of Rawlins's intentions.

He replies, "You got nothing to worry about anymore, baby. Nothing at all." Smiling, he tightens the scarf and in a matter of seconds gorgeous Pauline's life is over.

Blamed for the murder, Ernie sets out with Linda to prove his innocence, which he does. That he's cleared of any wrongdoing doesn't take away from the movie's taut-ness and toughness.

Payne is a convincing tough guy in the movie—so tough, in fact, that I bet his character has muscles in his lips.

GOING THE DISTANCE

In an interview several years after his title fight against Muhammad Ali, George Chuvalo had this to say: "To me it's kind of a negative. I lost the fight. So people see me and they say, 'Oh George, you went the distance with Muhammad Ali.' I say, 'No, he went the distance with me!'"

~*Richard Brignall*
Fearless

1

Read the prologue of Richard Brignall's *Fearless*, and you'll learn about Canadian heavyweight champion George Chuvalo's toughness in his 1967 fight, at Madison Square Garden, against Joe Frazier. The author writes that Frazier "had nearly punched an eye out of

George's head." When the fight was mercifully halted in the fourth round, Chuvalo was still on his feet.

Next, check out his 1970 fight against George Foreman at the Garden. "Foreman pounded on Chuvalo from the opening bell," Brignall writes. "Chuvalo could do nothing to stop the young boxer. The beginning of the end came one minute into the third round. Foreman crashed his left fist against Chuvalo's chin."

Did Foreman let up? Absolutely not. He "followed up with lefts and rights that drove Chuvalo's helpless body reeling around the ring.... Foreman was landing punches at the rate of about one per second. He kept this attack going for a full 40 seconds."

Finally referee Arthur Mercante stopped the slaughter.

2

When he was nineteen years old, with a record of eight wins and one defeat, Chuvalo, who hailed from Toronto, Canada, fought heavyweight contender Bob Baker of Pittsburgh, at Toronto's Maple Leaf Gardens, in 1957.

Baker won the decision. After the fight he visited Chuvalo in the Canadian's dressing room and told him he had nothing to feel ashamed about because what "beat you tonight," Baker said, "was my experience. You're going to beat a lot of guys and you're going to make a lot of money."

(At the Eastern Parkway Arena in Brooklyn in 1952, Baker outpointed journeyman New Jersey heavyweight Bill Gilliam. It was a close decision, and after the fight Baker told reporters Gilliam deserved the victory. Not only was Baker a good heavyweight, but also a man of excellent character.)

Chuvalo's first fight outside Canada was against Pat McMurtry in 1958, in a nationally televised fight at Madison Square Garden. At the end of ten rounds the more experienced McMurtry was awarded a unanimous decision.

A difficult loss for Chuvalo to accept.

But after a layoff of three months, Brignall writes that Chuvalo returned to the ring with "a new boxing teacher named Theodore McWhorter." The change worked and Chuvalo won four straight fights.

3

From 1985 to 1996 Chuvalo experienced several horrific family tragedies. One of his sons committed suicide, as did the fighter's wife Lynne. Two of his other sons died of drug overdoses.

"The deaths of three sons and his wife was almost enough to knock him down," Brignall writes. "He was still standing because he still had a lot to live for. This included a son [who became a teacher in the Toronto school system], a daughter, grandchildren, and new wife Joanne."

Brignall continues, "Tragic events pushed George's life in a new direction. He set out on a mission to describe how drugs took his family from him. He decided to travel across the country to spread his message about drugs. He has started his own organization, George Chuvalo's Fight Against Drugs. Instead of going to the gym, he went to schools, jails, and drug treatment centers."

4

Chuvalo fought from 1956 to 1978, compiling a 73-28-2 (64 KOs/2 KO'd by) record.

He was never knocked down.

In addition to the fighters previously mentioned, some of his opponents were—and it's an impressive list—Alex Miteff, Willi Besmanoff, Mike DeJohn, Doug Jones, Yvon Durelle, Zora Folley, Floyd Patterson, Ernie Terrell, Jerry Quarry, Muhammad Ali, Jimmy Ellis, Cleveland Williams, and Buster Mathis.

Take Chuvalo's title fight against Ali. They fought on March 29, 1966, at Maple Leaf Gardens and Chuvalo, a huge underdog, "made the greatest fight of his life," said Ali's trainer Angelo Dundee. "People ought to be proud of this man. I was, and I was in the other guy's corner."

In Jonathan Eig's biography *Ali*, the author writes, "Chuvalo finished the night with a lumpy face yet an unbroken spirit." In fact it was Ali who went to the hospital "because he was 'pissing blood' from so many kidney shots."

"Me?" Eig quotes Chuvalo as saying. "I got to go dancing with my wife."

JACK KEROUAC
AND THE WHIZ KIDS

The Philadelphia Phillies, aka the Whiz Kids, won their first pennant in thirty-five years, in the last game of the regular season, thanks to the heroics of Richie Ashburn, Dick Sisler, and Robin Roberts.

The date was Sunday, October 1, 1950. The place was Ebbets Field in Brooklyn. That's when Ashburn made a perfect throw to home, cutting off what would've been the game winning run for the Brooklyn Dodgers; when Sisler hit a dramatic top of the tenth inning homerun that put the Phillies ahead, 4-1; and when Roberts, without wavering, pitched for ten pressure-packed innings.

(Dick Sisler's father George was at the game, seated behind Philadelphia's dugout, standing and applauding and cheering as his son crossed home plate. Mobbed by his teammates, he waved and winked at his father, who was one of Major League baseball's greatest hitters. His lifetime batting average was .340. Ironically, George never won a pennant in his fifteen years as a big leaguer.

A few days after the Whiz Kids' win over the Dodgers, they went up against the powerful New York Yankees in the World Series.

They were defeated in four straight games.

Game 1, Shibe Park: Philadelphia's Jim Konstanty, later named the National League's Most Valuable Player, pitched a four-hitter, but New York's Vic Raschi was even better, hurling a two-hitter. Final score: 1-0, Yankees.

Game 2, Shibe Park: In the tenth inning some guy named Joe DiMaggio, a pretty good ballplayer, walloped a huge homerun to win it for the Bronx Bombers. Allie Reynolds was the winning pitcher and Robin Roberts, Philadelphia's ace hurler, the loser. Final score: Yankees 2, Phillies 1.

In Kurt Smith's article "Gene Kelly," in *The Whiz Kids Take the Pennant*, he quotes the Phillies' broadcaster as saying, "Joe hasn't got the ball out of the infield... in four trips. Roberts throwing.... A fly ball deep toward left field! This one may go all the way.... *A home run for Joe DiMaggio!*... Way out there into the upper tier in left-center field! A drive that took off — and stayed hit."

Game 3, Yankee Stadium: In relief of New York's Ed Lopat, Tom Ferrick was the winning pitcher, while Philadelphia's Russ Meyer took the loss. Final score: Yankees 3, Phillies 2.

Game 4, Yankee Stadium: The Yankees clinched the series with a 5-2 victory. Whitey Ford was the winning hurler; Bob Miller suffered the loss.

If Jack Kerouac had penned an essay for the book you're now reading—which I hope you're enjoying—it would have been titled

JACK KEROUAC

and the

Whiz Kids

and I'm positive here's what that renowned author would've written:

What if Philadelphia's second best pitcher lefty Curt Simmons 17-8 during the 1950 season had been declared eligible to pitch in the series?—Because his National Guard unit had been activated and though he was on a ten day pass during the World Series baseball commissioner Happy Chandler ruled him ineligible to play which didn't make sense, Simmons twenty one years old watched the games from a box seat, He was not a happy man—

What if Bubba Church an eight game winner during the '50 season and reliable in the clutch had not been injured?— September 15 was the day he was hurt and it was the top of the third inning, Church's first pitch a fastball was tagged by Cincinnati's Ted Kluszewski, It hit Bubba in the face, He spun around clutching his face and sank to his knees bleeding from his nose there was a gash underneath his left eye – (He was taken to a local hospital.) (Veteran pitcher Ken Heintzelman relieved him.)

Church was the Phillies' fourth best pitcher, Andy Seminick the team's catcher praised him as having great control and someone who doesn't seem to have much on the ball but each pitch he throws does something – What if Bob Miller an eleven game winner wasn't suffering at the end of the season from severe back spasms? What if he had been healthy?

I think the 1950 World Series might have had a different outcome –

Those players were a big part of the Whiz Kids' success in 1950 –

What I'm going to do now is prove to you I've been a baseball fan for many years, I'm going back to my Doctor Sax *novel, I'm going to quote Jack Duluoz its narrator who is (almost) me – Duluoz was probably ten years old back then, He loved baseball and the memory is vivid and even disturbing,* Dr. Sax *is I admit a strange novel and simultaneously about Duluoz's hugely fantastic inner and outer lives as he grows away from childhood which sometimes readers overlook – And here's what I wrote:*

"And there's me – playing my baseball game in the mud of the yard, draw a circle with a rock in the middle, for 3rd, for ss, 2nd base, first, for outfield positions and pitch ball in with a little selfward flick, a heavy-ball bearing, bat is a big nail, whap, there's a grounder between the rock of 3rd and ss, base hit into left.... the

diamond I'd drawn in the ground and the game I was playing were synonymous with regular distances and power-values in baseball, but suddenly I hit this incredible homerun with the small of the nail and drove the ball... sailing across the intervening stadium, or yard, into the veritable suburbs of the mythical city locating the mythical ballfield — into the yard of the Phebe Street house where we used to live — lost in the bushes there — lost my ball..."

I'm back, reader. The baseball game Duluoz/Kerouac created, probably the last one he played, was a defining event in his life because "a sinister end of the world home run had been hit" in a game that was "shrouded and foreboding and mysterious" and "put an end to childish play."

Kerouac, in the guise of Jack Duluoz, knows his childhood is over.

AND ESPECIALLY FOREMAN

*[George] Foreman alone among his blood broth-
ers got out alive. Frazier died poor and bitter. Ali
withdrew into his disease. But Foreman was left to
enjoy the spoils. He tootles around Houston, between
his ranch in Marshall with its herd of cattle, stallions,
and his home in Humble.... Or maybe he drifts over to
the church, or his youth center. He'd be driving his V-
12 BMW either way. Or writes a check for $1,000,007
to the M.D. Anderson Cancer Center.*

~Richard Hoffer
Bouts of Mania

Joe, You're the Champ

Boxing fans know that in their first meeting in 1971,
Joe Frazier defeated Muhammad Ali by decision.
Richard Hoffer, in his outstanding *Bouts of Mania:
Ali, Frazier, and Foreman — and an America on the Ropes*, a

book that should be read by everyone who loves the sweet science, quotes Ali as saying after the fight, "Don't call me the champ. Joe's the champ now," adding, in prescient fashion, "soon it will be old news."

As for Frazier, he was suffering from extremely high blood pressure and a kidney infection, and, Hoffer writes, "hustled off to a hospital in Philadelphia, where his bruised and depleted hunk lingered on and off for three weeks. "

More: "Frazier was in a state of mental and physical limbo, half comatose at times. Doctors eventually stabilized him and sent him on his way. But the undisputed champion of the world—the winner—had been mysteriously absent for his worldwide coronation, unexplainably unable to exploit his position."

Six days later Ali returned to the brash Ali of old. "Look at my face," he said. "Forget the bruise. Then go look at him, and you'll see who really won."

I was there. I saw the fight at the New Haven Arena, where it was screened. I'll say it again: I was there, along with five thousand fans, though the place was built for four thousand.

It was an experience and a memorable fight. Clearly Frazier won.

A Presence

By the time Frazier and Ali fought, George Foreman "was becoming, a heavyweight presence," Hoffer writes. His record was 26-0 (24 KOs).

Foreman and Frazier fought in Kingston, Jamaica, on January 22, 1973. The fight crowd gave the challenger little chance of winning, though there were several knowledgeable boxing people who thought differently. Hoffer quotes them:

Joe Louis: "[Frazier] is always in front of you and he's easy to hit."

Angelo Dundee, Ali's trainer: "I'm rooting for Frazier, but I've got this feeling Foreman will win. Why? Because he has all the attributes to beat Frazier's style. He's got a jab like I've never seen on a heavyweight since Sonny Liston. He has a strong left hand. I mean strong. He can stop a man in his tracks."

Howard Cosell: "There are going to be some shocked people in the world."

According to Hoffer, "Foreman was wary of Frazier," though he put on a confident act, "all the while wondering if he'd freeze in the ring. But he made it to the ring, stayed standing for referee Arthur Mercante's instructions, managed to return to his corner, and then entirely against his wishes the bell rang."

We know what happened next: Three knockdowns in the first round and three more in round two. After the last knockdown Mercante stopped the massacre. George Foreman was the new world heavyweight champion!

Later that evening Foreman was on his hotel balcony waving to a cheering crowd below. "But then," Hoffer writes, "he looked to the balcony next to his and recognized Joe Frazier's sister... and was immediately chastened. He waved an apology in her direction. He was apologizing for winning the heavyweight championship of the world."

"Don't feel bad, Mr. Foreman," she said. "We've had many victories."

Gonzo

In Hoffer's acknowledgements page he says the Ali, Frazier, and Foreman era might've been "the Golden Age of Sports writing. [It wasn't] a bad time to be reading boxing." To prove his point he cites several writers who covered the sport, among them Red Smith, Robert Lipsyte, Hugh McIlvanney, Jerry Izenberg, Norman Mailer, George Plimpton and Budd Schulberg.

Noteworthy, too, is what he writes about Gonzo journalist Hunter S. Thompson: Though he was sent to Zaire by *Rolling Stone* magazine to cover the Ali vs. Foreman fight, he believed writing about its president, the homicidal dictator Joseph Mobutu, would be more interesting to his readers than the Rumble in the Jungle. "Hobnobbing with his nibs [Mobutu], and all the generals standing around," Thompson said, "[was] the place to be."

But *what if* Thompson had written about the Battle in the Thicket? Imagine the interpretation he would've given it.

A WAVE FROM ANNE

The year was 1966 and Anne Bancroft had taken the role of Sabina in a two week off-Broadway production of Thornton Wilder's play *The Skin of Our Teeth*, which after six weeks of rehearsals would be performed at the Stockridge Theater.

A friend sent me the following letter many years ago involving the Oscar winning actress and the time he met her when she was staying in Lenox, Massachuetts, at Wheatleigh, an estate converted into a hotel.

(To be more accurate he met her from a distance.)

Here's what he wrote:

Anne Bancroft stayed at the hotel where I worked for the summer. She was acting in that Wilder play. She was picked up in a Buick probably by another actor for rehearsals every weekday morning. Nine-thirty. I don't know where the rehearsals were held. Probably at the theater in Stockridge. It wasn't far from the hotel. One morning before work a friend who worked at the hotel and me were tossing a football to each other on the hotel front lawn. There she was. She just came out of the hotel. She was about thirty or forty yards from us. We stopped tossing the ball and waved to her. We clapped too. She gave us that great Anne Bancroft smile. She waved to us. She bowed gently. Then she got into the car that was waiting for her and it drove off. We saw her maybe twenty-five times that summer. What I knew for certain was she enoyed our ritual as much as we did.

I told my friend how much I envied him and his Anne Bancroft experience. But I certainly didn't envy him, and I told him so, when about twelve years before meeting Anne he was given a tour of the Whalley Avenue Jail in New Haven.

He and two pals—all thirteen years old—decided to sneak into Roger Sherman grammar school in the early evening, in the fall, and check it out. They didn't take anything. Well, just a few No. 2 pencils, but they shouldn't have been in the school in the first place.

The evening janitor spotted them and called the cops. A squad car arrived and drove the three of them, handcuffed, off to jail, where the sheriff—no wardens back then in jails— uncuffed them, and he and a large guard immediately escorted the boys downstairs, where the cells were. Then the sheriff and the guard marched them up and down the narrow hall a few times for the inmates to gawk at.

The inmates cursed them with obscenities the boys never knew existed, tried to grab them, spat at them, and told them how sweet and juicy they looked.

Clearly white privilege didn't exist for the boys that evening.

"If you boys ever do what you did tonight again, I'll put you in a cell with some of the guys you just saw," the sheriff said, when they were back in his office. "I know you took only a few pencils but don't—mark my words—ever break into any place again."

The boys nodded meekly.

Tall and slim, probably in his early forties, clearly someone who took care of himself physically, the sheriff said, without raising his voice, "Now get out. Go home."

Guess what? Two weeks later I learned the sheriff had set the whole thing up beforehand. The inmates, all short-timers, were told to give the boys a harsh taste of what jail life might be like as they were paraded in front of them.

The strategy worked. My friend and his two pals never got into serious trouble again. Good for the sheriff. Good for them.

SAY MIKA FIVE TIMES

Before a capacity crowd at Madison Square Garden, on Friday, March 7, 2020, the New York Rangers' Mika Zibanejad did something remarkable. He scored—steady yourself!—five goals, as the Blueshirts defeated the powerhouse Washington Capitals in overtime, 6-5.

Traded from the Ottawa Senators to the Rangers in 2016, Zibanejad has been a prolific goal scorer for New York:

2016-17: 14 goals.

2017-18: 27 goals.

2018-19: 30 goals.

Before his performance against Washington, he had 33 tallies.

Commenting on what he did Friday night against Washington, the Swedish born six-two, 208-pound center said, "The puck followed me a lot today."

"He's got such a passion for the game," David Quinn, coach of the Rangers said. "He's everything you want in your best player. It's so important for an organization when you've got your best player approaching the game the way he does, not only in games but in practices."

Then there's Artemi Panarin. Zibanejad's fifth goal of the game, the *New York Post*'s Brett Cyrgalis writes, "was a breakaway set up by a brilliant pass from Panarin, who has not only lived up to the seven-year, $81.5 million deal he signed as a free agent this summer, but also has inserted himself into the conversation for the Hart Trophy as the league's Most Valuable Player."

"Having Zibanejad and Panarin on separate lines has made it much more difficult for teams to match up against the Rangers," Cyrgalis writes.

After reading about Zibanejad's marvelous feat, in my mind I went back to the late 1950s and a player for the Eastern Hockey League New Haven Blades named Fern Bernaquez. One Wednesday night during the 1961-62 season he scored six goals against the Johnstown Jets. After his sixth tally, he bowed deeply to the appreciative crowd that was on its feet cheering and applauding.

Back to the past again—specifically to 1962 and Madison Square Garden—where the great Bobby Hull of the Chicago Black Hawks skated the length of the Garden ice to score a goal against the New York Rangers.

Even diehard Ranger fans knew how special the goal was and were on their feet shouting their approval. (Compare Hull's rush to a football player running 110 yards for a touchdown.)

Also, there was what Dino Ciccarelli of the Washington Capitals did in 1989 against the Hartford Whalers at the Hartford Civic Center. The Washington winger recorded a pure hat trick, which is three straight goals. A unique achievement. Final score: Washington 8, Hartford 2.

THE WORD IS HOROWITZ

I'm often asked if I start writing a book without knowing the end. For me, it would be like building a bridge without knowing what it's got to reach.

~Anthony Horowitz
The Word is Murder

L ike Dr. John Watson, Sherlock Holmes's friend and biographer, Anthony Horowitz is the narrator of and a character in *The Word is Murder*. But Horowitz is also the author of *The Word is Murder*, while of course Sir Arthur Conan Doyle wrote the Holmes stories.

One of the most memorable scenes occurs near the end of the novel. Horowitz has discovered who the murderer is and they meet on what we'll call __'s home turf, and Horowitz is obviously going to be __'s next victim.

"__ knew I couldn't move," Horowitz writes. "__ must have put something in my coffee and I, fool that I was, had drunk it. Already I was screaming at myself. This was the __ who had strangled Diana Cowper and had sliced up her son. But why? And why hadn't I worked it out — hadn't it been obvious? — before I came here."

Horowitz is completely helpless and at __'s mercy.

To the rescue comes Daniel Hawthrone, an ex-London detective inspector who has enlisted Horowitz to join him as he investigates three murders and then write a book about him.

(Holmes, meet Watson. Watson, meet Holmes.)

With Hawthorne's arrival __ knows__ can't escape and there's only one thing __ can do. In one of the novel's most graphic and intense passages, __ "was standing in front of me," Horowitz writes, "no more than a couple of metres away. __ looked from Hawthorne back to me and I wondered what __ was going to do. I also saw the moment when __ made up __ mind. __ didn't put the scalpel down. Instead, __ lifted it to __ own throat, then drew it across in a single, decisive, horizontal slash."

As for the blunt and hotheaded, condescending and homophobic Hawthorne — he's brilliant, too — Horowitz rarely feels comfortable in his presnce and at times abhors him. (Who can blame him?)

But after he saves his life, Horowitz says, "I loved Hawthorne right then and my last thought before I passed out was how lucky I was to have him on my side."

Several days later Horowitz and Hawthorne engage in a conversation in the latter's apartment, and Horowitz suggests to the former DI that *The Word is Murder* should be the title of the book he's writing about him.

Horowitz: I thought that would make a good title. After all, I'm a writer, you're a detective. That's what it's all about.

Hawthorne: It'll do, I suppose.

Horowitz: You don't sound coinvinced.

Hawthorne: It's just a bit poncey. It's not something I'd read on the beach.

Poncey? The last time I came across that word was a year ago in Peter Robinson's novel *Many Rivers to Cross*. His main character, Detective Superintendent Alan Banks, is speaking with a chef, who we're told is "not at all the posturing prima donna in a poncey hat that Banks had expected."

SPEAKING OF THE PHILLIES

*T*he *Phillies Reader* will familiarize the reader with the many ups and downs of a major league baseball franchise. Edited by Richard Orodenker, the book contains a section devoted to the 1950 Philadelphia Phillies that includes essays by Ira Berkow and Ed Linn.

The excellent anthology, Orodenker writes, also "give[s] readers a sense of the varying styles that have marked baseball writing since since the late nineteenth-century..."

Despite the passage of time, and with it new interests, there are several baseball players who remain my favorites, and Eddie Waitkus is one of them. Bernard Malamud wrote about him in his 1952 novel *The Natural*, and in 1984 a film based on Malamud's novel was made starring Robert Redford, Glenn Close, and Robert Duvall.

Berkow's piece, "Eddie Waitkus," is about a tragic incident in the life of the smooth fielding, clutch hitting first baseman—Berkow calls his style "cool and buttery around the bag"—who played for the Philadelphia Phillies from 1949 to 1952.

In his essay we learn that in 1949 Waitkus, at the time a bachelor, was shot in his Chicago's Edgewater Beach hotel room by an insane nineteen-year-old named Ruth Ann Steinhagen.

"As time went on I just became nuttier and nuttier about [Waitkus]," she told Berkow, "and I knew I would never get to know him in a normal way" and "if I can't have him, nobody else can. And then I decided I would kill him."

Waitkus survied the shooting, returned to the lineup in 1950, played the entire season, batted .284, and won Major League Baseball's Comeback-of-the-Year honors.

That was also the year the Whiz Kids won their first pennant in thirty-five years, and Waitkus's steady play was one reason for their success.

Years after the shooting and Waitkus's retirement from baseball, Berkow received a letter from Waitkus's son, Edward (Ted) Waitkus, Jr., which was soon followed by several telephone conversations between the two men.

"The shooting changed my father a great deal," Ted Waitkus, a lawyer in Boulder, Colorado, told Berkow. "Before, he was a very outgoing person. Then he became paranoid about meeting new people, and pretty much stopped going out drinking with his teammates, which I guess they did in those days."

When the Waitkus family learned Steinhagen was going to be released from a mental hospital in the early fifties, "my father and my family fought to keep her in," Ted Waitkus said. "My father feared for his life."

In 1972, about twenty-three years after the shooting, Waitkus died. He was fifty-three years old.

For Ira Berkow, the shooting of Eddie Waitkus was a life-changing experience. He was nine years old when it happened. He writes, "The bullet that tore through the chest of Eddie Waitkus, the first baseman for the Philadelphia Phillies, ripped a hole through my idea that sports was not a part of real life, and that athletes were greater than mere mortals."

The two most significant points Ed Linn delivers in "The Tragedy of the Phillies," one of which is incorrect, are, first, his harsh claim that because of internal disciplinary problems, which began in 1949, "the [1950] Phils were as poor a ball club as ever won a pennant in a peacetime year."

Regarding the Phillies' World Series against the New York Yankees, Linn writes, "The kindest thing to do about [it] is to skip over it quickly."

(Linn conveniently doesn't mention the Whiz Kids lost games one, two, and three against a great New York team by one run.)

Second: Linn is spot on when he posits Philadelphia's owner Bob Carpenter "[ignored] the one new source of players opened up since the war, the source that was uncovered in 1946 when Branch Rickey signed Jackie Robinson."

It took nine years after the Brooklyn Dodgers signed Roy Campanella in 1948 before the Phillies signed their first African American, infielder John Irvin Kennedy.

Greg Erion, in his article "Game Four—1950 World Series," in *The Whiz Kids Take the Pennant*, quotes Richie Ashburn recalling that Campanella was interested in playing for the Phillies: "He once came to Shibe Park for a tryout," Ashburn said, "and they wouldn't even let him into the ball park. Can you imagine our club with Roy Campanella on it?"

REMARKABLE TURNAROUNDS

'm not exaggerating when I say hard punching Syracuse middleweight Joey DeJohn either knocked out his opponent or was knocked out by him.

And if you want proof, consider this: DeJohn began fighting professionally in 1944 and retired in 1952 with a record of 73-14-2. Fifty-one of his victories were by knockout, and he was knocked out ten times.

Some of his quality opponents were Bobby Dykes, Joe Rindone, Dick Wagner, Irish Bob Murphy, Ernie Durando, Norman Hayes, Robert Villemain, Lee Sala, and Jake LaMotta, all of whom, with the exception of Murphy, stopped him. (In 1952 DeJohn stopped Murphy.)

I saw DeJohn fight one time. It was against Norman Hayes, a tough middleweight from Roxbury, Massachusetts. The year was 1952, and the nationally televised fight took place at the Detroit Olympia.

Early in round two DeJohn hurt the twenty-one-year-old Hayes, but in the third round the accurate punching Hayes, who had lost rounds one and two, landed a left hook to DeJohn's body, followed by a right cross to his jaw. Down went the Syracuse fighter. Seconds after he was back on his feet he was hit by another left hook to the body, flooring him for the second time. When Hayes sent DeJohn to the canvas for the third time, referee Johnny Weber stopped the fight.

The *New York Times* writer covering the bout called the fight an "amazing reversal" for Hayes, and the *Boston Daily Globe*'s scribe said the win "was a great heart-warming victory" for the Roxbury middleweight.

In his dressing room after the bout, Hayes told reporters he was hit so hard in the first round he had no idea where he was until round three.

Hayes, who began fighting professionally in 1949 and retired in 1953, compiled a 25-17-1 (8 KOs/1 KO'd by) record. His best known opponents were DeJohn, Carl "Bobo" Olson (twice), Lee Sala, Ernie Durando, Jake LaMotta (twice), Laurent Dauthuille, Charles Humez, Paul Pender, and Robert Villemain.

One of his best efforts was the first time he fought future middleweight champion Olson in 1952 at the Civic Center, San Francisco. With the winner to face Sugar Ray Robinson, in defeat Hayes won the hearts of reporters and fans for, as one San Francisco sports journalist wrote, "[He] had reached deep inside himself, [which won] the admiration of the gallery. He had stuck in there when others of lesser mettle would have stepped out."

Another surprising turnaround occurred on December 12, 1951, when Kid Gavilan, fighting as a middleweight, fought Walter Cartier, in a nationally televised bout from Madison Square Garden.

It was one of the most memorable fights I ever saw. Cartier, who was ahead for nine rounds, used a sustained body attack to slow down the great Cuban. But in the tenth session Gavilan, not known as a heavy puncher, caught the Greenwich Village middleweight with a right cross to the jaw. Walter staggered. A barrage of punches followed. He collapsed to the canvas. Without counting, referee Ruby Goldstein signaled an end to the bout.

If you were a Gavilan fan, you were delighted that he turned the fight around, but if, like me, you rooted for Cartier, you were shocked at the contest's sudden turnabout.

Cartier's loss nearly broke my teenage heart.

Several years later sports journalist W.C. Heinz interviewed the long-retired Cartier for *Once They Heard the Cheers*. In his classic book on various athletes, Heinz tells us that four months before Walter's fight against Gavilan, Irish Billy Graham had out-boxed Gavilan in their welterweight title bout at the Garden.

The officials must've been watching a different fight, however, and awarded the decision to Gavilan. After the decision Graham was referred to by sports writers as "the uncrowned world welterweight champion."

Before the tenth round of Walter's fight against Gavilan began, Heinz told Irving Cohen, who managed both Cartier and Graham, "If [Walter] were my fighter, I'd tell him to go out and win the last round" — which Cohen and Charlie Goldman, Walter's trainer, did.

We know what happened.

"I think he had it won, and I'm sorry I gave you bad advice," Heinz later said to Cohen, who replied, "That's all right. It's just one of those things that happen now and then."

Also, Heinz tells us he had never apologized to Walter, and for years held himself responsible for the fighter's loss. His interview with Walter, the most memorable in the book, was his chance to make amends.

> Heinz: I'll tell you one fight that Walter didn't win and because of me.
>
> Mrs. Cartier: What one was that?
>
> Heinz: The Gavilan fight.
>
> Walter: You didn't lose me that fight. Walter Cartier lost it.
>
> Mrs. Cartier: How much time was left in the round?
>
> Walter: A minute, or a minute-and-a-half.
>
> Mrs. Cartier: I thought it was just seconds.

Walter: No, I've seen the pictures, and I was a little groggy, and I said to Ruby Goldstein, "Why don't you give me another knockdown?"

Heinz: And if it hadn't been for me, you'd have boxed that whole last round differently.

Walter: Only Walter Cartier lost that fight.

SPIRO'S PILES
AND MRS. DURRELL

Gerald Durrell's memoir *My Family and Other Animals* is about his eccentric family's life on the beautiful Greek island of Corfu (pre-WWII). A naturalist, conservationist, and zookeeper, he's the youngest of the Durrells and author of thirty-seven books.

A superb prose stylist, he's able to concentrate on a person, an animal, an event, and a place with detailed, vigorous clarity.

Like the excellent Masterpiece production starring Milo Parker as Gerald, Keeley Hawes as Louisa Durrell, Alexis Georgoulis as Spiro Halikiopoulos, Daisy Waterstone as Margo Durrell, and directed by Steve Barron and Roger Goldby, Durrell's book embodies a wonderful mix of smart British comedy and drama. It's the comedy I'm interested in because, as we speak, we're surrounded by everyday drama. Too much of it, in fact.

Consider the party the Durrell family decides to host. If you're wondering why, well, as Gerald explains, "As always, we had decided to give the party at a moment's notice, and for no other reason than that we suddenly felt like it."

And who's invited? "Overflowing with the milk of human kindness," Gerald continues, "the family had invited everyone they could think of, including people they cordially disliked."

There's a wonderful scene between Spiro, their best friend on the island and who I've come to think of as my mate, which happens when you really like a character in a work of fiction or non-fiction.

He arrives, but he's late and...

Spiro: Gollys, Mrs. Durrells, I'm sorry I'm lates.

Mrs. Durrell: That's all right Spiro. We were only afraid that you might have had an accident.

Spiro: Accidents. I never had accidents. No, it was them piles again.

Mrs. Durrell: *Piles?*

Spiro: Yes, I always gets them piles at this times.

Mrs. Durrell: Shouldn't you see a doctor if they're worrying you?

Spiro: Doctors? Whats fors?

Mrs. Durrell: Well, piles can be dangerous, you know.

Spiro: *Dangerous?*

Mrs. Durrell: Yes, they can be if they're neglected.

Spiro: I mean them aeroplane piles.

Mrs. Durrell: *Aeroplane* piles?

Spiro: Yes. French I thinks they are.

Mrs. Durrell: You mean aeroplane pilots.

Spiro: That's whats I says, piles.

And Finally

You gotta love Spiro, or Spiros as he calls himself, because the guy is funny without even trying.

Regarding Louisa Durrell, what's most memorable and admirable about her is she allows her family to be creative and eccentric. In turn, despite the chaos of her and her children's lives as they adjust to life on Corfu, they give her space to be herself — delightful and gracefully flaky.

SAL PARADISE'S REVELATIONS

J ack Kerouac's *On the Road* (1957) is a work of autobiographical fiction—that is, a mix of truth and bullshit. He was twenty-seven years old when he wrote it, and it's about his travels across America.

The book takes place between the years 1947 and 1950. In it he calls himself Sal Paradise.

Early on, Sal has a disturbing revelation. He wakes up one morning in Des Moines, Iowa, far from his Lowell, Massachusetts, home with "the sun reddening; and that was the one distinct time in my life, the strangest moment of all, when I didn't know who I was." He wasn't frightened, but "I was just somebody else, some stranger, and my whole life was a haunted life, the life of a ghost."

Written mostly in traditional prose, with occasional bursts of spontaneous prose, *On the Road* is a different book each time I read it, and this time it set me thinking about the time I taught an English Composition class at a local women's prison and used the passage you just read as a writing assignment for the eighteen students.

After I read it to the group I said, "Ladies, for next week write about a moment you came to a stunning revelation about yourself."

It worked. Their papers sparked a memorable discussion because they were personal, interesting, and above all honest. (You can count on inmates, if you ever teach a writing class in a prison, to write unabashedly honest papers.)

If I had to pick an essay to single out — which wasn't easy because they were all high quality — it was the one the students and I discussed the longest and most intensely after the author read it to the class.

I made a copy of it. Didn't edit it. Here are two excerpts: "My daughter is now six. I was in jail for four of the six years of her life. She will be ten when I get out. She's too young to understand now, so she loves me. When she gets older, she'll hate me. I didn't put her first; she'll hate me. I was a bad mother; she'll hate me."

Then she writes about her own mother and that, "I stopped hating her when I realized my daughter is going to hate me. My mother had many flaws but she was always there and she always loved me. Ironically, I feel my mother's pain and I dread the day when my daughter will hate me."

Later in the book Sal has another revelation. He and Marylou, the wife of Sal's close friend Dean Moriarty, are in San Francisco, living in a shoddy hotel on O'Farrell Street, and he thinks: "I had reached the point of ecstasy that I always wanted to reach, which was the complete step across chronological time, into timeless shadows, and wonderment in the bleakness of the moral realm, and the sensation of death kicking at my heels to move on...."

Anyway, near the end of the book Sal tells us about several great jazz musicians, and without exaggeration it stands alongside Kerouac's most revelatory, joyful, and breathless writing. There's "Louis Armstrong blowing his beautiful top in the muds of New Orleans [and] before him the mad musicians who had paraded on official days and broke up their Sousa marches into ragtime."

There's "swing, and Roy Eldridge, vigorous and virile, blasting the horn for everything it had in waves of power and logic and subtlety — leaning into it with glittering eyes and a lovely smile and sending out broadcast to rock the jazz world."

There's "Charlie Parker, a kid in his mother's woodshed in Kansas City, blowing his taped-up alto among the logs [and] coming out to watch the old swinging Basie and Benny Moten band that had hot lips Page and the rest — Charlie Parker leaving home and coming to Harlem and meeting mad Thelonious Monk and madder Gillespie — Charlie Parker in his early days when he was flipped and walked around in a circle while playing."

There's Lester Young, "that gloomy, saintly goof in whom the history of jazz was written; for when he held his horn high and horizontal from his mouth he blew the greatest and he wears his thick-soled shoes so that he can't feel the sidewalks of life his horn is held weakly against his chest... Here were the children of the American bop night."

"IT AIN'T YOUR NIGHT, TED"

Mike Stanton has written an absorbing biography about former heavyweight champion Rocky Marciano titled *Unbeaten: Rocky Marciano's Fight for Perfection in a Crooked World.* It's a book packed with old and new information about the former heavyweight king's life inside and outside the ring.

No matter how many times I read about Marciano's fight against the great Joe Louis, I'm always intrigued — and saddened. They fought October 26, 1951, at Madison Square Garden. It was one of those Gillette Blues Blades/ Friday Night Fights, so popular in the 1950s.

Nicknamed the Brockton Blockbuster, Marciano, as we know, scored an eighth round knockout over Louis, the once great former champion, ending what Stanton calls an "era."

Four months later in 1952 Rocky fought veteran Lee Savold at Philadelphia's Convention Hall. It was probably the most unimpressive outing of his career. Rocky's timing was way off and to say he almost missed as many punches as he landed isn't an exaggeration.

There was the infamous round six. Marciano, Stanton writes, "missed badly with a roundhouse right and fell flat on his face. Kneeling on the canvas with his hand on the rope, Rocky grinned up at Savold. Embarrassed and needing to redeem himself, Rocky got back on his feet and went after Savold. At the bell ending the round, Savold's manager leaped through the ropes and waved a towel to stop the fight."

Rocky looked much better several months later when he stopped tough Gino Buonvino, at the Rhode Island Auditorium, in two rounds. (In their first meeting in 1950, Rocky stopped Buonvino in the tenth round.)

In July, at Yankee Stadium, in one of his most impressive fights, he knocked out highly regarded Harry "Kid" Matthews in the second round. Two months later, in Philadelphia's Municipal Stadium, he became world heavyweight champion by knocking out Jersey Joe Walcott in round thirteen.

On April 27, 1957, Marciano retired from boxing with an unblemished record of 49-0-0, with 43 knockouts. On August 31, 1969, the night before his forty-sixth birthday, he died in a plane crash.

~~

Let's rewind to 1949 and Rocky's first fight against New Haven's Tiger Ted Lowry at the Rhode Island Auditorium. A seasoned veteran and spoiler, Lowry bewildered Marciano and clearly won the early rounds. Then, Stanton writes, "in the fifth, the fight strangely shifted. Lowry stopped attacking and retreated into a defensive shell. Rocky threw more punches than Lowry the rest of the way but had trouble connecting."

At one point in the fight, probably in the seventh or eighth round, Referee Ben Maculan became so annoyed with Lowry that he "warned [him] three times to start fighting."

Why did Lowry stop fighting? Was he exhausted because of his fast start? Did Rocky's body punches wear him down?

But if Lowry *deliberately* stopped fighting, what was the reason?

According to Stanton, "Lowry met shortly before the fight in his dressing room with a representative of Al Weill, who was not in Providence." He most likely told Ted, if I may speculate, *it ain't your night, Ted.*

As time passed Lowry shrugged off the idea that "he had agreed to lose in return for a guaranteed rematch when Rocky was a bigger contender and the payday would be larger. "

Lowry was ninety years of age when he died in 2010.

MORE THAN PRETENDING

...I sought peace of mind by reading, reading, reading. Books have always sustained me, especially when the blues blow through like a hurricane.

~*Val Kilmer*
I'm Your Huckleberry

1

Val Kilmer doesn't sound the way he once did, and that's because in 2015 he was a diagnosed with throat cancer. "The thing is," he writes in his memoir, the inimitable *I'm Your Huckleberry*, "when I speak now, I sound like Marlon Brando after a couple of bottles of tequila. It isn't a frog in my throat. More like a buffalo. It is difficult for others to understand what I am saying. My healing is steady, but so far, slow."

Writing for the *Washington Post*, Thomas Floyd says *I'm Your Huckleberry* — the title comes from a line Kilmer's Doc Holliday delivers twice in 1993's *Tombstone* — "offers a scatterbrained journey into [Kilmer's] idiosyncratic head space" but "you have to give it to him: He's playing by his own rules."

Consider the passage that might be the reason why Floyd believes Kilmer's memoir is "scatterbrained." After he writes about his experience playing Hamlet at the Colorado Shakespearean Festival in 1988, we read that "if I had my way my two grown children would live downstairs and I would sleep in my living room. I miss them every hour, even though I live so close to my daughter I can practically yell her name and she could hear me. I have to give them their space, but I don't want to."

His most poignant writing occurs when he says, "They are my greatest joy, my proudest achievement, even though it is painfully clear I have just about zero to do with their character. I admit it but I don't have to like it."

He ends the chapter with one flawless sentence: "Where were we?"

But before he wrote those heartfelt words about his daughter and son, Kilmer was writing about the characteristic he gave Hamlet — which was "confusion. I allowed Hamlet to be confused. In playing Hamlet I allowed myself to be confused."

Then three sentences later we're reading about Kilmer's children, which Floyd calls a "narrative detour" that makes Kilmer's writing "scatterbrained."

Scatterbrained? No! Too negative. A detour? Too inaccurate. What Kilmer did was make a writerly digression about, first, portraying Hamlet and, second, writing about his children.

2

Roger Zotti: Val, why do you write?

VK: I write for relief. I write for healing. I write to view the past more clearly and place myself firmly in the center of love. I want to get my story out as quickly as possible, but mostly I write because it feels good to share with the world what the world has shared with me.

RZ: You were relentless in perfecting your Jim Morrison character in 1991's *The Doors*. Your acting wasn't pretending to be Morrison. What you did was metamorphose into the group's late singer.

VK: I don't know if I have ever done it all the way like the others have done it for me, like, to name a few, Robert Downey Jr. (*Tropic Thunder*), Meryl Streep (*Sophie's Choice*) Hilary Swank (*Boys Don't Cry*) and Viola Davis in all of the performances she has given on TV and in movies.

RZ: You worked your ass off learning to sing in Morrison's baritone-tenor range, and at one point made two recordings and gave one to Oliver Stone, the movie's director, and another to the band's original members.

VK: One tape was me singing, the other was actually Jim. My gamble was to see if Stone and the Doors could tell who was who. When the time finally came, they couldn't tell us apart. I see my work in *The Doors* as one of the proudest moments of my career.

3

During filming of *The Doors* there was a disturbing incident that took place when Kilmer was singing a Doors song that upset Paul Rothchild, the longtime producer of the band's music, and he began screaming at Kilmer to stop singing.

VK: Hey man, all I'm saying is that this song is the dumbest, worst piece of filth I ever wrote and I don't want to sing it now or ever.

PR: Val, I'm serious. (Visibly upset) Stop it! This is too much. I just can't.

VK: I'm really sorry, Paul. I won't talk in his dialect anymore. It's just there's so little time and for me the best way is just—

PR: No, no, no. It's not that. It's... It's... It's what you are saying. I don't know who told you those things about the song but [Jim] said them only to me, and I've never told anyone. So I just need you to stop for a while.

Eerie.

A lifelong Christian scientist, Kilmer explains that "somehow, through all the months and months of studying [Morrison], his interviews and video, and talking to his friends and reading all his girls' manuscripts about their time with him, somehow I was able to like the same things he liked — or in this particular case didn't like."

Think back to what Kilmer said early in his memoir about the characters he portrays in his movies: "I was and was not the character I played. The character went through me, and therefore was me, even as I went through the character and became him. Pieces of me and pieces of him merged."

That Kilmer didn't receive an Oscar for his work in *The Doors* and *Tombstone* (1993), where he became Jim Morrison and Doc Holliday, is a fricking shame.

NEVER UNDERESTIMATE
A REFEREE

Sammy and Humberto

The Night the Referee Hit Back, the title of award-winning boxing historian Mike Silver's latest book, refers to what happened on January 27, 1970, when a welterweight from Panama named Humberto Trottman took a swing at fifty-four-year-old referee Sammy Luftspring in the sixth round of his fight against Clyde Gray.

Apparently Mr. Trottman was dissatisfied with Mr. Luftspring's officiating.

What he didn't know was that the Canadian-born Luftspring was a former professional prizefighter. A competitive welterweight, Luftspring, from 1936 to 1938, won 23 of 27 fights. One of those victories, a thirteen-round knockout of Frankie Genovese, earned him the Canadian welterweight championship.

When Luftspring moved to New York City in 1939, Silver points out, "Al Weill became his manager and Whitey Bimstein his trainer."

He retired in 1940 with a 31-8 (13 KOs) record and in 1985 was inducted into the Canadian Boxing Hall of Fame.

In Silver's 2014 article about the Trottman fight he quotes Luftspring, who, in his 1975 autobiography *Call Me Sammy*, wrote: "What was going on in my head was that I was in a boxing ring with a boxer who had just thrown one punch and probably intended to give me a sample of a few more. How I ever managed, purely by instinct, to dodge his right I will never know. But I had no intention of letting it be unreturned." Luftspring fought back "and the next thing I knew, I had popped him three or four more times without getting touched again myself."

Hemingway, Silver, and Stillman's Gym

In Ernest Hemingway's *A Moveable Feast*, the author takes you to Paris in the 1920s, where you'll visit, to name just one of many popular gathering places, the Shakespeare and Company bookstore owned by Sylvia Beach. According to Hemingway, Beach was "kind, cheerful and interested, and loved to make jokes and gossip."

Hemingway said he was "very shy when I first went into the bookshop, and I did not have enough money on me to join the rental library." But Beach trusted him and "made out a card and said I could take as many books as I wished."

The advice she gave him before he left her store with an armful of books was, "Don't read too fast."

You'll also meet F. Scott Fitzgerald, his wife Zelda, Ezra Pound, Ford Madox Ford, and Gertrude Stein.

Consider what Hemingway writes about Fitzgerald and Zelda: "He would start to work and as soon as he was working well Zelda would begin complaining about how bored she was and would get him off to another drunken party. They would quarrel and then make up and he would sweat out the alcohol on long walks with me, and make up his mind that this time he would really work, and would start off well. Then it would start all over again."

In seventy-four words Zelda is revealed to be the direct opposite of Sylvia Beach.

My point is that in *A Moveable Feast,* Hemingway's artistry puts you, the reader, right *there* in Paris. And when those people he writes about converse with him, it's as if they're speaking to you too.

Turning back to Mike Silver, one of today's most knowledgeable and trustworthy boxing writers. In *The Night the Referee Hit Back*'s marvelously and evocatively written autobiographical opening chapter, "Boxing in Olde New York: Unforgettable Stillman's Gym," Silver does what Hemingway did when he wrote about Paris. His writing expertise places you right *there* inside Stillman's by evoking the gym's smells: "... a combination of liniment, stale cigar smoke, leather, and sweat."

The gym's sights: "You could spend hours at Stillman's just looking at the interesting faces of some of the characters who always showed up. I had never seen so many dented noses in one place. Half the guys standing around, whether fighters, trainers, or managers, had mugs that could have filled the cast of a *Guys and Dolls* production."

And its sounds: "A cacophony echoed through the gym: the rhythmic *rat-a-tat-tat* of the speed bags; jump ropes slapping against the hardwood floor; the thump of leather-covered fists hitting the heavy bags, and, if hit hard enough, the jangling sound of the chains that bolted them to the ceiling; fighters snorting and grunting as they shadowboxed and threw punches at imaginary opponents."

... the jangling sounds of the chains that bolted [the heavy bags] to the ceiling. That's a memorable and powerful image!

For Silver, "Walking into Stillman's was like entering a time warp. I felt like I had suddenly found myself in an old black-and-white movie. All my senses were engaged in taking it all in." Stillman's was the place, you see, where Silver began his education in the sweet science and he has never forgotten its "magic and allure. I thank my lucky stars I was able to experience it."

(It's a statement similar to what Hemingway once said to a friend: "If you are lucky enough to have lived in

Paris as a young man, then wherever you go for the rest of your life, it stays with you.")

Tiger Ted

A compilation of twenty-eight articles Silver wrote over the past forty years, *The Night the Referee Hit Back* also contains several terrific interviews. One of them is with Silver's friend Tiger Ted Lowry and another with the great Archie Moore.

Lowry grew up in New Haven, Connecticut, and graduated from Troup Junior High School, which has a personal meaning for me and a friend, retired lawyer Stu Rosen of South Windsor, Connecticut. In 2008, we met Lowry at the Connecticut Boxing Hall of Fame Induction ceremony, at Mohegan Sun Casino in Uncasville, Connecticut. He was one of the year's inductees.

It was a reunion of sorts. Stu and I were also graduates of TJH many years after Lowry's class graduated. A pleasant surprise. We chatted about our days at the school and about its enormous playground, where at least three or four softball games always seemed to be taking place.

Lowry fought from 1939 to 1955 and compiled an interesting record of 70-68-10 (35 K0s.) Wait! Sixty-eight losses! "Ted lost count of the number of hometown decisions that went against him," Silver explains. "At least half of those 68 losses could just as well have gone the other way. He took those losses in stride and accepted them as the cost of keeping busy and earning a steady income."

But it was a different matter when Lowry went up against "a top contender," Silver points out, "and he had nothing to lose and everything to gain, he became what he always could have become and let loose with the full measure of his talent."

Two examples: In his 1948 fight against the great Archie Moore, he gave the Old Mongoose fits for ten rounds, though he lost the decision. Later Moore admitted Lowry was one tough, savvy hombre!

There was Lowry's 1952 fight against light heavyweight champion Joey Maxim. "Maxim was scheduled to defend his title against the great Sugar Ray Robinson," Silver writes. "There was no way the powers in charge would allow Ted Lowry to get the decision and put a damper on that big fight." (Of course, Maxim was awarded the decision.)

In his interview with Lowry, Silver asked him how Muhammad Ali would've fared against the great Joe Louis. "I think Joe Louis would have knocked him out," Lowry said. "Joe was the type who stayed right on you and it would be hard for Ali to outbox him, and if Joe hit him, it would be terrible. Joe did not back up. He was always dangerous with the left hand or right hand, it made no difference."

Asked by Silver if he thought "Muhammad Ali was a great fighter," Lowry said, "No. He moved too much for me. But he was a good boxer. Good boxer. But I don't think that at the time he was fighting, the top-notch fighters were around."

In his interview with former light heavyweight champion Archie Moore, whose 194-23-20 (132 KOs/7 KO'd by) is astounding, Silver asked him who was the greatest fighter pound-for-pound he ever saw. Moore pondered the query for "about ten seconds," then said, "Henry Armstrong. Here is a man who won the featherweight, lightweight, and welterweight titles all in the same year, and the men he beat to win those titles were great fighters in their own right."

Like his other two books, *The Arc of Boxing: The Rise and Decline of the Sweet Science* and *Stars in the Ring: Jewish Champions in the Golden Age of Boxing*, Silver's *The Night the Referee Hit Back* is skillfully written, brimming with informed insights about how boxing was, is, and probably will be.

SIMPLY THE GREATEST

Don't specialize in one sport. Do what you enjoy doing. Work hard, practice, but have fun. Don't limit yourself to one sport.... If you don't have fun playing the sport, don't do it.

~Joan Joyce
Connecticut Softball Legend

Achievements

A 753-42 win-loss record, a 35-0 record in 1975, and an earned run average of 0.09 are just several of Joan Joyce's many accomplishments during her twenty-six-year fast pitch softball career.

And let's not forget she struck out about 10,000 batters.

If you enjoy having your mind boggled — and I do — check out pages 153 to 159 in Tony Renzoni's precisely written and much needed biography of Joyce for more of her achievements.

Titled *Connecticut Softball Legend Joan Joyce* (The History Press) and enhanced by photographs of her family, friends, teammates, and Joyce herself, Renzoni's book is a tribute to the greatest female athlete ever, an athlete he rightly believes "deserves to be a household name."

And when you finish reading it, your conclusion will be, I'm sure, as the author points out, "Joan Joyce is a champion of women in sports, and has propelled the national profile of women athletics for generations to come."

Renzoni pays close attention to why Joyce hasn't been given the recognition she deserves. One reason "is the media was completely different when Joan played sports." Specifically, "[Joyce] received newspaper coverage across the U.S. but very little TV or radio recognition." Another reason is that "Joan never believed in promoting herself like some of her contemporaries and today's athletes. She always let her accomplishments speak for themselves. I admire her for this. She is loved and respected by her teammates, other athletes, fans, and students. Joan, for many years, has been an inspiration for young girls (and boys)."

And if you're wondering what prompted Renzoni to write a book about Joyce, it happened after a conversation with his friend Joe Marra. Both men were born and raised in Waterbury, Connecticut, and, Renzoni writes, "we had the good fortune of watching Joan pitch a number of times. Like so many other fans, we were in total awe of her. After my conversation with Joe, I thought to myself, 'Hey, this is a great story to tell in a book.'"Marra agreed.

What Renzoni hopes readers take from his book, which is available at amazon.com and Barnes & Noble, is "the true recognition [Joan] deserves and to make people aware of the greatness of this amazing player, coach and teacher. Young girls especially should be encouraged to learn more about Joan, since she has been a major champion of women in sports." He adds that readers "will have a better understanding of why Joan Joyce [is] respected and loved by so many throughout her entire career. Joanie is the most amazing person I ever met! It is my belief that there will never be another athlete like Joan Joyce."

(Joyce also excelled in bowling, golf, basketball, and volleyball, which Renzoni discusses in Chapters 13 and 14.)

Joan and Ted

Joyce pitched against Ted Williams of the Boston Red Sox, one of Major League baseball's all-time greatest hitters, "several times in the early 1960s," Renzoni writes, "and Williams couldn't hit her."

On August 5, 1966, Joyce and Williams faced each other for the final time before a sell-out crowd at Waterbury's Memorial Stadium. "But once again Williams was unable to hit any of Joyce's pitches. Except for a couple of foul tips."

Question: How did Williams react to his encounters with Joyce on the ballfield?

Answer: Generously! "[He] was in awe of Joan's talent and sang her praises in a December 30, 1999 article by Tom Yanz of the *Hartford Courant* newspaper," Renzoni writes. The man called Teddy Ballgame—what a great nickname!—said, "Joan Joyce was a tremendous pitcher, as talented as anyone who ever played."

(Williams once told a friend that the toughest pitcher he ever faced was a teenager named Joan Joyce.)

In addition to facing Williams, Joyce pitched to major leaguers Hank Aaron and Paul Blair. She struck out the great Aaron, while Blair of the Baltimore Orioles batted against her on December 21, 1975, in Rotunda, Florida, and fared no better than Williams and Aaron—no surprise—though "he did manage to foul off a few."

Sixty Years

And aside from her softball career with the Raybestos Brakettes and Connecticut Falcons, writes Renzoni, "Joan refereed for 34 years, was a college golf coach for 18 years, and is currently Head Coach of the Florida Atlantic University women's softball team (for the last 25 years). Joan has been coaching for 60 years!"

Carpenter Joan

Renzoni's interviews with Joyce appear at the end of *Connecticut Softball Legend Joan Joyce*, and in one of them and she fondly recalls the time she became—yes—a carpenter. When she was twelve years old, she lived on Tudor Street in Waterbury, and "I actually helped a fellow build a house," she told Renzoni. "I was walking by, and the guys were building a house, about three or four houses up the street."

She asked one of the carpenters if he needed help and "it ended up that it was this seventy-five-year-old carpenter and myself who built the house. I did everything. I put roofs on, I put tiles in the bathrooms, everything. And so, my parents ended up buying the house that the guy and I built."

Another notable experience in her youth involved her mailman, Tony Marinaro, who also pitched for the Waterbury Bombers. "In the summertime," Joyce said, "I used to go up to the top of the hill to help him deliver. In return, he would spend about twenty minutes with me to teach me softball. Tony Marinaro actually was the one that told me about the Raybestos Brakettes."

Did I mention Joyce pitched 150 no-hitters and 50 perfect games?

AUTHOR'S NOTES

The boxing essays in *Jack Kerouac and the Whiz Kids* were originally published in slightly different versions in the *International Boxing Research Organization Journal*.

Many thanks to Dan Cuoco, the *Journal*'s editor and publisher, for sending me information about the Chico Vejar vs Eddie Compo and Norman Hayes vs Joey DeJohn fights. Thanks are extended to my wife Maryann for her suggestions regarding many of the essays. I'm grateful to Tony Renzoni for his recommendations about the Joan Joyce piece, "Simply the Best." Kudos to Maynard Strickland for suggesting the title of the "It Ain't Your Night, Ted" essay.

Various sources differ slightly regarding Archie Moore's amazing record as a professional boxer. I went with boxrec.com.

As for Duk Koo Kim, one source referred to him as Kim Duk-koo. I stayed with Mark Kriegel's spelling of the late fighter's name in his biography of Ray Mancini, *The Good Son*.

ABOUT THE AUTHOR

Born in New Haven, Connecticut, Roger Zotti graduated from Eastern Connecticut State College in 1966 and later received his Master's Degree from Wesleyan University in 1971.

He taught adult education at several Connecticut correctional centers for over twenty years, retiring in 1993. A regular contributor to the *IBRO Journal*, he also serves on its editorial board. He is a member of the Connecticut Boxing Hall of Fame Induction Committee, and facilitates a movie class for Adventures in Lifelong Learning in Norwich, Connecticut.

His interests are hockey, running, stationary biking, boxing, WNBA, movies (old and new), and music.

He, his wife, and their innovative dog live in Preston, Connecticut. They have two adult children, Tom and Leslie.

Contact him at rogerzotti@aol.com to praise this book.